ng a New Career

on
Technology

The Field Guides to Finding a New Career series

Advertising, Sales, and Marketing

Arts and Entertainment

Education

Film and Television

Food and Culinary Arts

Health Care

Information Technology

Internet and Media

Nonprofits and Government

Outdoor Careers

Information Technology

By Amanda Kirk

Ferguson Publishing
An imprint of Infobase Publishing

Field Guides to Finding a New Career: Information Technology

Ferguson
An imprint of Infobase Publishing
132 West 31st Street
New York, NY 10001

Library of Congress Cataloging-in-Publication Data

Kirk, Amanda.
  Information technology / by Amanda Kirk.
    p. cm. — (Field guides to finding a new career)
  Includes index.
  ISBN-13: 978-0-8160-7601-7
  ISBN-10: 0-8160-7601-4
  1. Information technology—Vocational guidance. 2. Electronic data processing personnel—Vocational guidance. I. Title.
  T58.5.K57 2009
  004.023—dc22
                          2009015311

Ferguson books are available at special discounts when purchased in bulk quantities for businesses, associations, institutions, or sales promotions. Please call our Special Sales Department in New York at (212) 967-8800 or (800) 322-8755.

You can find Ferguson on the World Wide Web at http://www.fergpubco.com

Produced by Print Matters, Inc.
Text design by A Good Thing, Inc.
Illustrations by Molly Crabapple
Cover design by Takeshi Takahashi

Printed in the United States of America

Bang PMI 10 9 8 7 6 5 4 3 2 1

This book is printed on acid-free paper.

Contents

Introduction: Finding a New Career   vii

How to Use This Book   ix

Make the Most of Your Journey   xi

Self-Assessment Quiz   xv

Chapter 1   Computer Programmer   1

Chapter 2   Database Administrator   12

Chapter 3   Computer Systems Analyst   22

Chapter 4   Computer Software Engineer   33

Chapter 5   Computer Repair Technician   44

Chapter 6   Cyber Security Specialist   54

Chapter 7   Network Administrator   64

Chapter 8   Systems Engineer   75

Chapter 9   Forensic Computing Specialist   86

Appendix A   Going Solo: Starting Your Own Business   97

Appendix B   Outfitting Yourself for Career Success   111

Index   123

Introduction: Finding a New Career

Today, changing jobs is an accepted and normal part of life. In fact, according to the Bureau of Labor Statistics, Americans born between 1957 and 1964 held an average of 9.6 jobs from the ages of 18 to 36. The reasons for this are varied: To begin with, people live longer and healthier lives than they did in the past and accordingly have more years of active work life. However, the economy of the twenty-first century is in a state of constant and rapid change, and the workforce of the past does not always meet the needs of the future. Furthermore, fewer and fewer industries provide bonuses such as pensions and retirement health plans, which provide an incentive for staying with the same firm. Other workers experience epiphanies, spiritual growth, or various sorts of personal challenges that lead them to question the paths they have chosen.

Job instability is another prominent factor in the modern workplace. In the last five years, the United States has lost 2.6 *million jobs*; in 2005 alone, 370,000 workers were affected by mass layoffs. Moreover, because of new technology, changing labor markets, ageism, and a host of other factors, many educated, experienced professionals and skilled blue-collar workers have difficulty finding jobs in their former career tracks. Finally—and not just for women—the realities of juggling work and family life, coupled with economic necessity, often force radical revisions of career plans.

No matter how normal or accepted changing careers might be, however, the time of transition can also be a time of anxiety. Faced with the necessity of changing direction in the middle of their journey through life, many find themselves lost. Many career-changers find themselves asking questions such as: Where do I want to go from here? How do I get there? How do I prepare myself for the journey? Thankfully, the Field Guides to Finding a New Career are here to show the way. Using the language and visual style of a travel guide, we show you that reorienting yourself and reapplying your skills and knowledge to a new career is not an uphill slog, but an exciting journey of exploration. No matter whether you are in your twenties or close to retirement age, you can bravely set out to explore new paths and discover new vistas.

Though this series forms an organic whole, each volume is also designed to be a comprehensive, stand-alone, all-in-one guide to getting motivated, getting back on your feet, and getting back to work. We thoroughly discuss common issues such as going back to school, managing your household finances, putting your old skills to work in new situations, and selling yourself to potential employers. Each volume focuses on a broad career field, roughly grouped by Bureau of Labor Statistics' career clusters. Each chapter will focus on a particular career, suggesting new career paths suitable for an individual with that experience and training as well as practical issues involved in seeking and applying for a position.

Many times, the first question career-changers ask is, "Is this new path right for me?" Our self-assessment quiz, coupled with the career compasses at the beginning of each chapter, will help you to match your personal attributes to set you on the right track. Do you possess a storehouse of skilled knowledge? Are you the sort of person who puts others before yourself? Are you methodical and organized? Do you communicate effectively and clearly? Are you good at math? And how do you react to stress? All of these qualities contribute to career success—but they are not equally important in all jobs.

Many career-changers find working for themselves to be more hassle-free and rewarding than working for someone else. However, going at it alone, whether as a self-employed individual or a small-business owner, provides its own special set of challenges. Appendix A, "Going Solo: Starting Your Own Business," is designed to provide answers to many common questions and solutions to everyday problems, from income taxes to accounting to providing health insurance for yourself and your family.

For those who choose to work for someone else, how do you find a job, particularly when you have been out of the labor market for a while? Appendix B, "Outfitting Yourself for Career Success," is designed to answer these questions. It provides not only advice on résumé and self-presentation, but also the latest developments in looking for jobs, such as online resources, headhunters, and placement agencies. Additionally, it recommends how to explain an absence from the workforce to a potential employer.

Changing careers can be stressful, but it can also be a time of exciting personal growth and discovery. We hope that the Field Guides to Finding a New Career not only help you get your bearings in today's employment jungle, but set you on the path to personal fulfillment, happiness, and prosperity.

How to Use This Book

Career Compasses

Each chapter begins with a series of "career compasses" to help you get your bearings and determine if this job is right for you, based on your answers to the self-assessment quiz at the beginning of the book. Does it require a mathematical mindset? Communication skills? Organizational skills? If you're not a "people person," a job requiring you to interact with the public might not be right for you. On the other hand, your organizational skills might be just what are needed in the back office.

Destination

A brief overview, giving you and introduction to the career, briefly explaining what it is, its advantages, why it is so satisfying, its growth potential, and its income potential.

You Are Here

A self-assessment asking you to locate yourself on your journey. Are you working in a related field? Are you working in a field where some skills will transfer? Or are you doing something completely different? In each case, we suggest ways to reapply your skills, gain new ones, and launch yourself on your new career path.

Navigating the Terrain

To help you on your way, we have provided a handy map showing the stages in your journey to a new career. "Navigating the Terrain" will show you the road you need to follow to get where you are going. Since the answers are not the same for everyone and every career, we are sure to show how there are multiple ways to get to the same destination.

Organizing Your Expedition

Fleshing out "Navigating the Terrain," we give explicit directions on how to enter this new career: Decide on a destination, scout the terrain, and decide on a path that is right for you. Of course, the answers are not the same for everyone.

Landmarks

People have different needs at different ages. "Landmarks" presents advice specific to the concerns of each age demographic: early career (twenties), mid-career (thirties to forties), senior employees (fifties) and second-career starters (sixties). We address not only issues such as overcoming age discrimination, but also possible concerns of spouses and families (for instance, paying college tuition with reduced income) and keeping up with new technologies.

Essential Gear

Indispensable tips for career-changers on things such as gearing your résumé to a job in a new field, finding contacts and networking, obtaining further education and training, and how to gain experience in the new field.

Notes from the Field

Sometimes it is useful to consult with those who have gone before for insights and advice. "Notes from the Field" presents interviews with career-changers, presenting motivations and methods that you can identify with.

Further Resources

Finally, we give a list of "expedition outfitters" to provide you with further resources and trade resources.

Make the Most of Your Journey

With computers becoming more indispensable to business, government, and our private lives, information technology—often referred to as IT—is a discipline that is only going to grow and diversify. Thirty years ago the idea of widespread cybercrime and the need for computer security were nearly unimaginable, as would have been the idea of a full-time job writing software applications for mobile phones. Both of these fields are burgeoning today, however, employing thousands of workers trained in computer science at colleges, universities, and technical institutes. Putting IT in this perspective, it is impossible imagine the IT careers that will be commonplace 20 years from now as technology further changes the way we do business and manage our personal lives, finances, and schedules. The growing ubiquity of computers is the advantage to a career in IT; the disadvantage is the constant need to keep one's skills up-to-date. Continuing education is a must in all IT disciplines, although the specific skills and certifications needed vary by position.

The most basic job title that comes to mind in the IT-verse is probably computer programmer. The non-technological amongst us tend to think of anyone who works with computers as a computer programmer. In fact, this job title refers specifically to those IT professionals who write computer code. Computer programmers use mathematical languages that must be learned just as one learns any foreign language. This is one of the most technical of techie jobs: "behind the scenes" even to those tech workers who are normally thought of as "behind the scenes," such as software designers and system administrators. If you are interested in highly technical and largely solitary work, this may be the career for you.

Some IT professionals must bridge the IT/business divide in their everyday work, and these types of IT jobs require a mix of technical, business, and communication skills. Database administrators design, develop, maintain, secure, troubleshoot, and update the database applications that private, public, and nonprofit sector organizations use to store data. They work closely with the end users of the databases to ascertain their needs, adapt existing databases to new business uses, and take advantage of cutting-edge technological innovations. Network administrators also work with the end users of a connected set of computers in a business environment. They must be able to interact with and respond to the needs of business users and provide them with technical support and training. Network administrators need strong technical skills in the fundamentals of setting up, maintaining, and securing computer networks, but they also need excellent communication skills to manage network support staff and interact with network users.

The network administrator may have some assistance in providing security for the computer network from cyber security specialists. This unique profession involves maintaining the privacy and integrity of data stored in computer databases and other types of software programs. Cyber security is particularly important to government, the military, and the financial sector, but it is an issue for all computer users. Hackers are an ever-increasing threat, as are viruses and other malware that can compromise and even destroy important computer data. Cyber security specialists must be expert hackers themselves, always able to stay one step ahead of the bad guys.

In that respect, cyber security specialists are similar to, and often work closely with, forensic computing specialists. Professionals in this growing IT specialty are usually employed by local, state, or federal law enforcement agencies but can also serve as independent consultants or be associated with law firms or private companies. Their job is to find digital evidence that can be used in criminal prosecutions and civil cases. Television shows that have dramatized the field of forensics have generated intense interest in forensics-related careers. Computers are increasingly used to store and transmit information related to criminal activity and are also used to commit cybercrimes. The ability of skilled forensic computing specialists to obtain hidden or deleted information on suspect computers is crucial to successful prosecution of both cybercriminals and lower-tech criminals who simply have incriminating information related to their crimes stored on their computer equipment. The real work of forensic computing specialists is not always as glamorous and dramatic as portrayed on television, but it is certainly an exciting profession for an IT aspirant with the requisite hacking skills and law enforcement training and background.

If you are looking for a challenging IT career that will enable you to combine technical, design, and problem-solving skills, you might want to consider computer software engineering or computer systems analysis. Software engineers work in teams (although some smaller-scale and independent designers work alone) to design the software programs that are essential to every type of computer use. Computer programmers usually code the designs, but some software engineers do their own coding. Thus the mix of skills needed for this job include most of the programming languages needed by a coder, accompanied by an ability to assess end user needs and to work in a coordinated team environment. Computer systems analysts perform a similar design function except that they design computer systems to meet user specifications instead of designing software applications. This role calls for an in-depth understanding of platforms and operating systems, as well as a knack for translating business needs into technical requirements.

If you like approaching IT work from a systems perspective, and you want something even broader than computer systems design, you might want to consider becoming a systems engineer—especially if you come to IT work from an engineering background. Systems engineers usually start out with an education in one of the traditional engineering disciplines, such as electrical, mechanical, civil, or aerospace/aeronautics, and develop an interest in overseeing complex engineering projects while working in their field. Systems engineers, like several of the IT professions in this volume, must possess both technical and business-related skills, especially communication and project management expertise. Systems engineers are essentially project managers who work on highly complex projects. Their unique abilities lie in using special tools to ensure that every step of a complex project, such as building a space station, a bridge, or even a complex software application, is undertaken in the correct order and carefully coordinated with all of the other steps in the entire life cycle of the project. Systems engineers have a big-picture focus, yet they also must be obsessively detail-oriented. It is a uniquely challenging career and a relatively recent addition to the engineering repertoire. Courses are available at the undergraduate level, but this is a career you can move into if you are an engineer with project management experience and you are willing to invest in some continuing education and certification courses.

Last, but by no means least, there is one IT career that does not fit into a neat category with any of the others, but stands alone. This is computer repair technician. A computer repair technician combines the tinkering aptitude of a watchmaker with the patience of a saint. As the name implies, computer repair technicians are called upon to help individuals and businesses when a computer problem brings work to a screeching halt. The problem can be a virus, a mysterious hard drive crash, a software bug, a cup of coffee spilled on the keyboard, a guinea pig in the server, or it can be the old bane of the technical support specialist: the failure of the user to properly read the manual. Whatever the cause of the computer malfunction, it is up to the repair technician to sooth the nerves and salve the ego of the anxious computer user while addressing the problem with speed, tact, and a sensitivity to privacy. Computer repair technicians do not often earn as much as other IT professions, but neither do they need the same educational qualifications. Most employers simply want to see that job applicants are good at repairing computers and do not particularly care how they acquire those skills. On- the-job training is important in all IT disciplines, but it is especially relevant for repair technicians. This is not true for most other IT careers in this volume, where specific education and experience requirements may impede your ability to transfer swiftly into your newly desired IT role. Do not be discouraged as the chapters in this volume will provide you with information on how to acquire the necessary qualifications to forge a path into your new IT career.

All of the jobs in this volume will appeal to the career changer who loves working with computers and solving technical problems. Each job has unique aspects that will enable it to match up with diverse professional and educational backgrounds. Whether your background is in business, engineering, law enforcement, the military, project management, or in a specific scientific or technical industry, one of these careers should enable you to capitalize on your existing qualifications. If you are interested in exploring whether an IT career might be right for you, read on for more specific information about each profession mentioned in this introduction.

Self-Assessment Quiz

I: Relevant Knowledge

1. How many years of specialized training have you had?
   (a) None, it is not required
   (b) Several weeks to several months of training
   (c) A year-long course or other preparation
   (d) Years of preparation in graduate or professional school, or equivalent job experience

2. Would you consider training to obtain certification or other required credentials?
   (a) No
   (b) Yes, but only if it is legally mandated
   (c) Yes, but only if it is the industry standard
   (d) Yes, if it is helpful (even if not mandatory)

3. In terms of achieving success, how would rate the following qualities in order from least to most important?
   (a) ability, effort, preparation
   (b) ability, preparation, effort
   (c) preparation, ability, effort
   (d) preparation, effort, ability

4. How would you feel about keeping track of current developments in your field?
   (a) I prefer a field where very little changes
   (b) If there were a trade publication, I would like to keep current with that
   (c) I would be willing to regularly recertify my credentials or learn new systems
   (d) I would be willing to aggressively keep myself up-to-date in a field that changes constantly

5. For whatever reason, you have to train a bright young successor to do your job. How quickly will he or she pick it up?
    (a) Very quickly
    (b) He or she can pick up the necessary skills on the job
    (c) With the necessary training he or she should succeed with hard work and concentration
    (d) There is going to be a long breaking-in period—there is no substitute for experience

II: Caring

1. How would you react to the following statement: "Other people are the most important thing in the world?"
    (a) No! Me first!
    (b) I do not really like other people, but I do make time for them
    (c) Yes, but you have to look out for yourself first
    (d) Yes, to such a degree that I often neglect my own well-being

2. Who of the following is the best role model?
    (a) Ayn Rand
    (b) Napoléon Bonaparte
    (c) Bill Gates
    (d) Florence Nightingale

3. How do you feel about pets?
    (a) I do not like animals at all
    (b) Dogs and cats and such are OK, but not for me
    (c) I have a pet, or I wish I did
    (d) I have several pets, and caring for them occupies significant amounts of my time

4. Which of the following sets of professions seems most appealing to you?
    (a) business leader, lawyer, entrepreneur
    (b) politician, police officer, athletic coach
    (c) teacher, religious leader, counselor
    (d) nurse, firefighter, paramedic

5. How well would you have to know someone to give them $100 in a harsh but not life-threatening circumstance? It would have to be...
   (a) ...a close family member or friend (brother or sister, best friend)
   (b) ...a more distant friend or relation (second cousin, coworkers)
   (c) ...an acquaintance (a coworker, someone from a community organization or church)
   (d) ...a complete stranger

III: Organizational Skills

1. Do you create sub-folders to further categorize the items in your "Pictures" and "Documents" folders on your computer?
   (a) No
   (b) Yes, but I do not use them consistently
   (c) Yes, and I use them consistently
   (d) Yes, and I also do so with my e-mail and music library

2. How do you keep track of your personal finances?
   (a) I do not, and I am never quite sure how much money is in my checking account
   (b) I do not really, but I always check my online banking to make sure I have money
   (c) I am generally very good about budgeting and keeping track of my expenses, but sometimes I make mistakes
   (d) I do things such as meticulously balance my checkbook, fill out Excel spreadsheets of my monthly expenses, and file my receipts

3. Do you systematically order commonly used items in your kitchen?
   (a) My kitchen is a mess
   (b) I can generally find things when I need them
   (c) A place for everything, and everything in its place
   (d) Yes, I rigorously order my kitchen and do things like alphabetize spices and herbal teas

4. How do you do your laundry?
   (a) I cram it in any old way
   (b) I separate whites and colors

(c) I separate whites and colors, plus whether it gets dried

(d) Not only do I separate whites and colors and drying or non-drying, I organize things by type of clothes or some other system

5. Can you work in clutter?
(a) Yes, in fact I feel energized by the mess
(b) A little clutter never hurt anyone
(c) No, it drives me insane
(d) Not only does my workspace need to be neat, so does that of everyone around me

IV: Communication Skills

1. Do people ask you to speak up, not mumble, or repeat yourself?
(a) All the time
(b) Often
(c) Sometimes
(d) Never

2. How do you feel about speaking in public?
(a) It terrifies me
(b) I can give a speech or presentation if I have to, but it is awkward
(c) No problem!
(d) I frequently give lectures and addresses, and I am very good at it

3. What's the difference between *their, they're,* and *there*?
(a) I do not know
(b) I know there is a difference, but I make mistakes in usage
(c) I know the difference, but I can not articulate it
(d) *Their* is the third-person possessive, *they're* is a contraction for *they are*, and *there is* a deictic adverb meaning "in that place"

4. Do you avoid writing long letters or e-mails because you are ashamed of your spelling, punctuation, and grammatical mistakes?
(a) Yes
(b) Yes, but I am either trying to improve or just do not care what people think

(c) The few mistakes I make are easily overlooked
(d) Save for the occasional typo, I do not ever make mistakes in usage

5. Which choice best characterizes the most challenging book you are willing to read in your spare time?
(a) I do not read
(b) Light fiction reading such as the Harry Potter series, *The Da Vinci Code*, or mass-market paperbacks
(c) Literary fiction or mass-market nonfiction such as history or biography
(d) Long treatises on technical, academic, or scientific subjects

V: Mathematical Skills

1. Do spreadsheets make you nervous?
(a) Yes, and I do not use them at all
(b) I can perform some simple tasks, but I feel that I should leave them to people who are better-qualified than myself
(c) I feel that I am a better-than-average spreadsheet user
(d) My job requires that I be very proficient with them

2. What is the highest level math class you have ever taken?
(a) I flunked high-school algebra
(b) Trigonometry or pre-calculus
(c) College calculus or statistics
(d) Advanced college mathematics

3. Would you rather make a presentation in words or using numbers and figures?
(a) Definitely in words
(b) In words, but I could throw in some simple figures and statistics if I had to
(c) I could strike a balance between the two
(d) Using numbers as much as possible; they are much more precise

4. Cover the answers below with a sheet of paper, and then solve the following word problem: Mary has been legally able to vote for exactly half her life. Her husband John is three years older than she. Next year,

their son Harvey will be exactly one-quarter of John's age. How old was Mary when Harvey was born?
(a) I couldn't work out the answer
(b) 25
(c) 26
(d) 27

5. Cover the answers below with a sheet of paper, and then solve the following word problem: There are seven children on a school bus. Each child has seven book bags. Each bag has seven big cats in it. Each cat has seven kittens. How many legs are there on the bus?
(a) I couldn't work out the answer
(b) 2,415
(c) 16,821
(d) 10,990

VI: Ability to Manage Stress

1. It is the end of the working day, you have 20 minutes to finish an hour-long job, and you are scheduled to pick up your children. Your supervisor asks you why you are not finished. You:
(a) Have a panic attack
(b) Frantically redouble your efforts
(c) Calmly tell her you need more time, make arrangements to have someone else pick up the kids, and work on the project past closing time
(d) Calmly tell her that you need more time to do it right and that you have to leave, or ask if you can release this flawed version tonight

2. When you are stressed, do you tend to:
(a) Feel helpless, develop tightness in your chest, break out in cold sweats, or have other extreme, debilitating physiological symptoms?
(b) Get irritable and develop a hair-trigger temper, drink too much, obsess over the problem, or exhibit other "normal" signs of stress?
(c) Try to relax, keep your cool, and act as if there is no problem
(d) Take deep, cleansing breaths and actively try to overcome the feelings of stress

3. The last time I was so angry or frazzled that I lost my composure was:
   - (a) Last week or more recently
   - (b) Last month
   - (c) Over a year ago
   - (d) So long ago I cannot remember

4. Which of the following describes you?
   - (a) Stress is a major disruption in my life, people have spoken to me about my anger management issues, or I am on medication for my anxiety and stress
   - (b) I get anxious and stressed out easily
   - (c) Sometimes life can be a challenge, but you have to climb that mountain!
   - (d) I am generally easygoing

5. What is your ideal vacation?
   - (a) I do not take vacations; I feel my work life is too demanding
   - (b) I would just like to be alone, with no one bothering me
   - (c) I would like to do something not too demanding, like a cruise, with friends and family
   - (d) I am an adventurer; I want to do exciting (or even dangerous) things and visit foreign lands

Scoring:

For each category...

For every answer of *a*, add zero points to your score.
For every answer of *b*, add ten points to your score.
For every answer of *c*, add fifteen points to your score.
For every answer of *d*, add twenty points to your score.

The result is your percentage in that category.

Computer Programmer

Computer Programmer

Career Compasses

Get your bearings on what it takes to be a successful computer programmer.

Relevant knowledge of programming languages (50%)

Organizational skills to keep up with your workload (20%)

Mathematical skills are an asset in understanding programming languages (20%)

Ability to manage stress is key to handling the pressure of deadlines and inevitable glitches in your programs (10%)

Destination: Computer Programmer

To the uninitiated, computers can seem either sentient or magical. Whether the task you give your computer is simple, such as calculating the sum of two plus two, or is a staggeringly complex physics problem, computers today can possess such sophisticated logical structures for problem solving that they have given rise to the term *artificial intelligence.* The truth, though, is that there is always a "man behind the curtain." It is people—specifically, computer programmers—who create

these logical structures and write them in a format that the computer can interpret.

No matter how bright it seems, the computer is merely doing what it is programmed to do. Computer programmers write the code that gives the computer instructions what to do in a given situation, and in every possible permutation of that situation. It is an exacting task, and after a program is written it has to be tested to make sure it works as planned. Programmers sometimes engage in this testing themselves, but it can also be conducted by specialized software testers who are more like end users than programmers in their understanding of the computer's infrastructure. Likewise, it is rarely the programmer who decides what the program that they are coding will do. Programmers usually follow directions from software designers, engineers, and analysts, who work with end users to find out what functionality they need. When problems are detected with new programs, programmers have to debug them, testing and re-testing their work until the problem is solved. Repairing code is a critical task, but it is also important that programmers modify and update old programs, adding new functionality based upon changing user needs and new technological developments. As you have probably noticed, it is rare for a software program to remain in use without periodic updates.

There are two main types of computer programmers: systems programmers and application programmers. The former is a broader category, the latter more specific. Systems programmers work with operating systems (the connection between how software programs communicate

Essential Gear

Know thy code and keep it fresh. If you are considering a career in programming, you should already be well aware that programming languages evolve on a daily basis, and new ones are written that make old ones quickly obsolete. Being able to demonstrate to potential employers that you are keeping yourself abreast of the latest developments in the field, and continually updating your skill set, is key to finding employment. The more languages you know, the more jobs, obviously, are open to you. Objected-oriented languages like C++ and Java are as essential today for virtually all programmers as are the more conventional programming languages like COBOL. If you specialize in systems and database programming, you should know as many of the languages associated with these programming areas as possible, such as DB2, Oracle, and Sybase.

with each other, and with peripheral devices). They make sure an entire computer system is connected, and have extensive knowledge of how each job is performed. Applications programmers write individual software programs to perform specific tasks. They may have to consult with a systems programmer to make sure that software programs can "talk" to each other within a given computer system.

Programming code are special languages that the computer can "read," The languages that computers speak are fundamentally different from the languages we speak. The structure of computer languages is more like a mathematical equation than a sentence, which is one reason that an aptitude for math comes in handy for programmers. There are too many computer languages in use today to list them all here. Some of the major ones include COBOL, an older, conventional programming language; Prolog, a so-called artificial intelligence language; and Java and C++, which are versatile object-oriented languages used frequently on the Web and in the gaming industry. Programmers sometimes specialize in one language, but they usually are familiar with several. It is growing more common to concentrate on one type of programming, such as for databases or the Web, rather than a specific language. This is because languages change so frequently and environments like the Web call for multiple languages.

Another way that programming is changing is that software is coding itself. Yes, you read that correctly. Computer-assisted software engineering (CASE) is helps programmers to automate the coding process for some projects, enabling coders to focus their valuable time and energy on more complex and specific tasks. Another way for programmers to dispense with more routine aspects of coding is to use a code library, which provides databases of sections of code for common functions.

Essential Gear

Do not be shy about showing off. Some potential employers will demand samples of your work, but whether they ask or not, it is a good idea to provide examples of programs or Web sites that you have coded. You can put programs on disks and include Web site URLs on a separate sheet with your résumé. If you are applying for a job online, mention in your cover letter that samples of your work are available, and ask them in what format they would like to receive them. Pick your most polished projects that have the "cleanest" code and, when possible, choose projects that reflect the type of work you would like to do.

This saves programmers time because they do not have to reinvent the click wheel with every new program they write. In addition to CASE, computer programmers often work in teams with other technicians, especially if the project is large. Only very small pieces of software can be written efficiently by one programmer: Most projects are done in teams, with each programmer assigned a specific piece based upon his or her expertise.

If you are looking to change careers into a growing field, computer programming is not one of them. Despite the fact that computers are becoming more ubiquitous in the lives of people around the globe, jobs in programming are actually declining and expected to continue to decline slightly (about 4 percent, according to the Bureau of Labor Statistics) over the next decade. One of the advantages of this line of work is its portability—you can telecommute from anywhere with an Internet connection. Yet this characteristic has the downside that programming jobs are some of the most easily outsourced abroad. Do not let this deter you if you have a strong aptitude and interest in this field. There will continue to be programming jobs available, and one of them could be yours if you have the relevant skills. Job prospects will be best for those who possess at least a bachelor's degree rather than a two-year degree and/ or certificate, and who are fluent in numerous programming languages. Although you do not want to spread yourself so thin that your language skills lack depth, you can never know too many programming languages if you want to advance in the field.

Another aspect of the job of computer programmer to consider is the work environment. Programmers, as you would imagine, spend a lot of time indoors seated at a computer terminal in an office. As noted above, this can be a home office, but the sedentary nature of the work is still a factor to take into account. Programmers usually work regular 40-hour weeks, but looming deadlines can mean occasional long hours and stressful periods when a new product is in the final stages of testing. Programmers sometimes work with technical writers to develop the manuals that will go to end users, which can be an unwelcome aspect of the job for some. If you want to connect with other programmers and learn more about the field from those already in it, check out some of the online message boards on Web sites geared toward programmers. A good one to try is Dream.In.Code, a programming and Web development community, found at http://www.dreamincode.net.

You Are Here

You can begin your journey to Computer Programmer from a few different locales.

Do you have technical aptitude and a detail-oriented approach to work? As anyone who has written a program knows, one misplaced character can cause it not to run. In order to write accurate programs that will function as intended, you will need to be attentive to the smallest details in your code. A typo in a business report might go unnoticed and have no effect on the success of the project at hand; a typo in a line of code effectively negates all of your hard work. Translating the ideas of non-technical business staff into software that is simple and effective from the end users' standpoint requires a high degree of technical acumen. You may be told, "I need a program that does X" and have to make it a reality. To be a successful computer programmer requires a native technical ability to translate ideas into lines of code, and the willingness to focus on the details.

Do you have a related degree or work experience? Making the journey from a non-technical, totally unrelated employment history is not going to be easy, unless your hobby has been writing code in your spare time. Potential employers will look at your degree: Do you have at least a bachelor's degree? Is it in computer science or a related field like mathematics or engineering? Have you used technical skills in previous jobs? In short, how can you convince a potential employer to take a chance on someone who is making a career change to move into this field? They will want to know not only that you can do the work, but also that you are a better choice than other applicants who have been computer programmers all along. As you begin your excursion down this new career path, think of ways that your existing degree and work experience could be harnessed to pull you along your desired road.

Do you like learning new skills? No matter if you are familiar with every operating system and programming language in the known universe, you can count on new ones being developed in the near future. There will also be extensions and modifications of existing languages and systems that will require you to study and take continuing education classes to keep

Navigating the Terrain

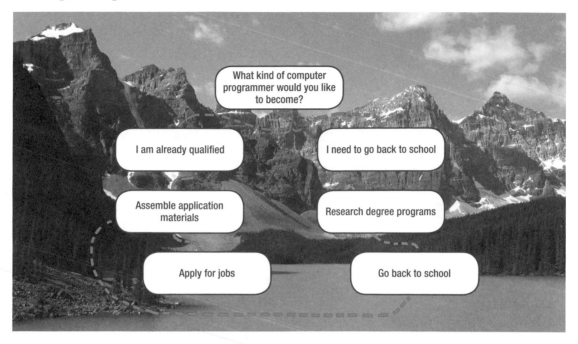

your technical skills up to date. There is no resting on your laurels in the world of computer programming. Your next program better do what its last iteration did, and more, all with a more streamlined and user-friendly interface. If the idea of revisiting and revising your old work does not appeal to you, you might want to rethink programming as a career move.

Organizing Your Expedition

Before you set out, know where you are going.

Decide on a destination. This may seem like an obvious question but starting with it may yield some useful and surprising insights: Why do you want to be a computer programmer? Do you enjoy the technical aspects of designing software? Is it a hobby of yours to design games or widgets or other downloadable programs? Perhaps you find yourself thinking of ways that the software you use for your job could be improved. Whatever motivates you to change careers and try programming

Stories from the Field

John Grand
Peter Jay Weinberger
Computer programmer for Google
Mountain View, California

It has often been noted that there is a close relationship between mathematics and computer science. In fact, computer science is a part of the Department of Mathematics at many universities. It has also been said many times that a roadblock in one career path can send one's footsteps down a more successful avenue. Examples abound of famous people who were fired from one gig only to get their big break on the next one. Peter Weinberger has some familiarity with that phenomenon. He received his Ph.D. in mathematics from the University of California, Berkeley, specializing in analytic and algebraic number theory. He studied with Derrick Henry Lehmer and his dissertation was entitled "Proof of a Conjecture of Gauss on Class Number Two." He worked for a year in Washington, D.C., then taught mathematics at the University of Michigan, Ann Arbor, but was denied tenure—a major setback in his academic career. He might have gotten tenure at another university, but when faced with the prospect of living someplace

for a living can serve as a guide to what kind of programmer you want to be. Consider also the different programming languages and operating systems used for different types of programs. If prefer to work in a Web-based environment and find databases boring, you should look for jobs that call for Java rather than Oracle skills.

Scout the terrain. Starting with the links at the end of this chapter, investigate what programming jobs are available in your locale, and take a shrewd look at the qualifications for those jobs. Your background may provide you with some relevant expertise. A previous career in health care could help you relate to the needs of companies that program software for health care services, and help you upgrade to a first class position. What sort of certification courses are available in your locale? Which local that did not appeal to him, he left academia and got a job at AT&T Bell Labs in New Jersey. At AT&T Weinberger first worked on computer databases but later transferred into research. His claim to fame is his part in the development of the AWK programming language. The AWK (pronounced "auk") programming language was a forerunner and inspiration for later programming languages such as Perl. AWK processes text-based data in the form of files or data streams using string data type, associative arrays, and regular expressions. It is a cross-platform language used as the standard scripting language in the Unix operating system. Following his discoveries with AWK, Weinberger was promoted to head of computer science research at AT&T. He soon moved on to become chief technology officer at Renaissance Technologies, and currently works as a software engineer for Google.

Weinberger laid the groundwork for his career transition at the University of Michigan, where be learned the FORTRAN and C programming languages. He was fortunate in that Michigan had a sophisticated computer environment in the late 1960s. His dissertation advisor had been an early adopter of computers, so he was set on that path from his student days to combine programming with mathematics. The central lesson of his career is that one can always build on and branch out from his or her existing educational and work experiences.

schools have a good track record in placing students in real jobs? Do you live in an area with a large number of programming jobs? Could you telecommute to your job of choice? This is increasingly an option, and it expands the available pool of jobs considerably. You could search the globe for a suitable job without leaving your office.

Find the path that's right for you. Computer programming does not take place in a vacuum. The programs that you create are used by people in virtually every employment field imaginable to carry out their work. While it is not strictly necessary for the programmer to have any affinity with the end user's field, it certainly helps. Not only will it make the work more interesting for you, but also you may have the opportunity to bring your insights to bear on the design of your programs to increase their utility. With that in mind, consider your current area of expertise, as well as your interests, as you search for a programming job.

Go back to school. Most programming jobs will require a minimum of a bachelor's degree. There are some jobs for which a two-year associate's degree coupled with appropriate certifications and experience will suffice, but a four-year degree is a necessary foundation for upward mobility in the field. This degree does not have to be in computer programming but could be in a related information systems field or mathematics. A business or hard sciences degree will also translate well into a career in computer programming, provided appropriate supplementary courses are taken. What undergraduate major is ideal for your job depends on the type of industry for which you program. Those that do programming for the financial arena, for example, would look favorably on a degree in finance, whereas engineering firms might prefer applicants with an engineering background. A master's degree is not a necessity for most programming jobs if you want to stick with programming itself, but those looking to move up and into a supervisory role could find an MBA useful. There are a select number of applied programming jobs for which a master's degree is required. As always, look at the specific requirements of positions that interest you and plan your return to school accordingly.

Landmarks

If you are in your twenties . . . You may be well situated to acquire useful educational prerequisites for a career in programming. If you do not yet have a bachelor's degree, go back to school and major in computer science. If you have your bachelor's already in another field, look at the educational requirements in ads for jobs that you would like and take the appropriate courses at a technical or community college, or enroll for a master's.

If you are in your thirties or forties . . . Much of the advice for those in their twenties still applies. You want to begin by looking at the requirements for your desired position, and work from there finding the appropriate classes available locally or online. You may be able to get tuition reimbursement from your current employer if you are in a related field.

If you are in your fifties . . . A lot depends upon whether you are making a move from a related field or a completely unrelated line of work. If related, see if your current employer will accommodate your class schedule for continuing education or provide partial or full tuition reimbursement. If you are hoping to make the leap from a different line of work entirely, consider joining some professional networking organizations to make connections in your new field.

If you are over sixty . . . This career move is not going to be an easy one if you are not already working in a related field. Potential employers are unlikely to view the résumé of someone over sixty who is completely new to computer programming favorably. In this case, be sure to emphasize samples of your work to impress employers, and highlight your most up-to-date language skills. If you are already in a related field, and can demonstrate strong, relevant technical skills, then age should not be much of an issue.

Further Resources

Jobs for Programmers is exactly what it sounds like: a Web site where you can search for programming jobs using various criteria, and post your résumé. http://www.prgjobs.com

National Workforce Center for Emerging Technologies is based at Bellevue Community College in Washington State. It provides professional development information such as continuing education, workshops and consulting services. http://www.nwcet.org

IEEE Computer Society is a division of the Institute of Electrical and Electronics Engineers and is the largest organization of computing professionals. Its membership benefits include access to a large digital library. http://www.computer.org

Association for Computing Machinery is a professional membership organization for programmers and related computer science fields that provides many online resources, including a digital library. http://www.acm.org

Database
Administrator

Database Administrator

Career Compasses

Get your bearings on what it takes to be a successful database administrator.

Relevant knowledge of database software (50%)

Organizational skills because you are, after all, managing a database (20%)

Mathematical skills are absolutely essential for this career choice (20%)

Ability to manage stress is a useful quality to possess, not just in the IT-verse, but also in any professional environment (10%)

Destination: Database Administrator

If you are keen to become a database administrator (DBA), odds are that you already work in IT. The good news is that segueing into database administration is one of the easier career changes to make within the IT field. There is more good news: This is a growing field. One cannot say any field is recession-proof, but the world is now organized into databases, and they have to be managed by someone. Why not you?

Businesses have always kept information such as inventory, customers, vendors, and financial and personnel records in databases; libraries have always listed their books; and schools have always listed their courses and kept records of students and alumni. The government maintains many databases, too, on everything from budgetary information to voter registration. Charities keep track of donors and recipients of aid. The public, private, and nonprofit sectors could not function without a staggering number and variety of databases to keep track of virtually every piece of information used in their work. In fact, the address label on most of the mail that you receive comes from a database of one sort or another.

Once upon a time, these databases were kept on paper, in filing cabinets or catalogs, like the old card catalog at your local library. The electronic age brought with it both new means to store information and, thanks to the Internet and e-commerce, more information to store. For many older people, their first experience with an electronic database was when their local library switched to an electronic card catalog. For some of us, the transition was made reluctantly, with much grumbling, but now most of us have become so used to carrying around databases in our pockets, such as the contacts in our mobile phones, that we cannot imagine living without them. Today, if your library's online catalogue does not have the book you want, you can search the databases of libraries worldwide and have the book ordered via interlibrary loan and delivered to your local branch—and get an e-mail notifying you when the book has arrived. The library will have your e-mail address stored in a database. If you do not finish it by the due date, you can renew it online, tapping into yet another database. Where does it end? It does not: Our lives are organized, stored and managed by databases.

Essential Gear

Pack your problem-solving skills. There is a stereotype of IT employees that they lack people skills, which is why they are comfortable sitting hunched over a computer screen all day, mucking about with lines of code. This common perception is not true of database administrators, who must have excellent communication skills to work with the end users of their database. They must be able to think logically and be adept problem-solvers. Every new user need is a problem waiting to be solved. It will be your job to come up with a viable solution. The end user often will be unaware of technical limitations and will ask you to make the database do something that you know to be technologically and logistically challenging. You need to be able to make it happen.

Let us look at one more example to see how pervasive databases are in our lives. When you purchase groceries, each item scanned at the register sends a notification to another database that there is one less of that item in stock. The stock database may communicate with the supplier database without human involvement in the process, and a delivery truck may show up with more of the items that are running low without a clerk placing an order manually. The store also maintains a database of your purchases, which might calculate loyalty reward card points and print out coupons geared to your shopping habits, not to mention the connection to a database at your bank when you swipe your card to pay that tracks how much money you have and where and how much is being spent.

Database administrators are responsible for making sure that all of these types of databases perform the functions that are needed of them, and that they work properly and keep their information secure. These IT professionals work with the end users of the database to ascertain their needs—what, exactly, the database is supposed to do, who will be using it, and how they need it to function. The database administrator must listen to users and set up a system that addresses their needs, then they must test it until all of the bugs are worked out and the users are satisfied with the software. They must also handle periodic upgrades to the database and make modifications to it based upon changing user needs.

Security is a major responsibility of database administrators, who are usually the gatekeepers of access to databases. They have administrative privileges and define access levels for other users, issuing logins and passwords. The security of the data is extremely important to an employer, and it is essential for the legal privacy purposes for many types of data. Some data may be jealously guarded from competitors, whether it contains client names and addresses or trade secrets. The integrity and security of a database is one of the main responsibilities of a database administrator, as is the safety of the data from loss as well as theft. All data must be backed-up, a practice that you may have routinized on your home computer. A database administrator will also have standard back-up procedures, just on a larger scale.

There is a hierarchy within the field of database administration, as in most jobs, and entry-level database administrators may earn less than $50,000 per year and find themselves relegated to doing the grunt work such as routine coding, testing, user education, running back-ups, and even data entry. Higher-level database administrators can make six-figure salaries. The variety of work will depend upon the size of the employer and the sophistication of their database needs. Most database administrators work in teams with programmers and database managers. The IT department is usually completely separate from the business side, which can sometimes impede communication of user needs. Recently there has been an increasing tendency for employers to seek out IT workers with business training, especially in managerial roles. Database design is, strictly speaking, a separate function from database administration. However, depending upon the company, much database development work may be assigned to database administrators. On a related note, database administrators have to provide development and testing support to programmers. Again, depending upon the company, this can form a large part of the job.

You Are Here

You can begin your journey to database administration from a few different locales.

Do you have a bachelor's degree in computer science, information science or management information systems? If not, you are going to need to get one, as this is the minimum educational requirement for a database administrator position. You may be able to parlay strong related work experience into an offer even if your degree is in a different field. There are also some lower-level jobs that may accept an associate's degree in an IT discipline, but these may not offer advancement and may be little more than glorified data-entry clerk positions.

Are you detail-oriented? If not, you need to seriously consider whether this is the right field for you. Think about it: One typo can throw off an entire series of data. Data entry fields are often defined by punctuation marks so that a misplaced comma could cause a print run of 100,000 address labels to all print without zip codes on them, leaving you with a very angry boss.

Do you mind sitting at a computer all day? If you are reading this, you are likely already an IT professional of some sort, and you are probably used to spending a lot of time at your computer for both work and pleasure. But it is still worth mentioning that database administrators do not have much of an offline component to their jobs. If you are a supervisor or a database designer, you may participate in meetings, but most of the time you will be sitting at your PC, which if you do not take care of yourself can lead to poor posture, obesity, eye and back strain, and a variety of repetitive stress injuries to the wrists and hands.

Organizing Your Expedition

Before you set out, know where you are going.

Decide on a destination. Databases are just computer software programs that are customized for different business environments. With so many on the market today, no single database administrator could know them all, so you will need to specialize. If you are not sure which program to pick, bear in mind that you cannot go wrong with Oracle,

Navigating the Terrain

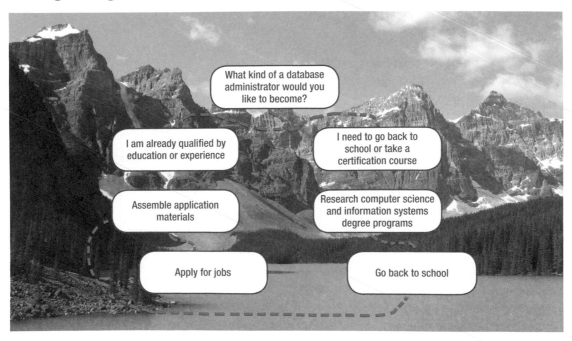

What kind of a database administrator would you like to become?

I am already qualified by education or experience

I need to go back to school or take a certification course

Assemble application materials

Research computer science and information systems degree programs

Apply for jobs

Go back to school

Notes from the Field

Joel Robertson
Freelance Oracle database designer
Chicago, IL

What were you doing before you decided to change careers?

I was the network administrator for a hospital (medical) supply company in the western suburbs of Chicago.

Why did you change your career?

My wife ran her own business and she needed a database to keep track of information. I thought designing it would be an interesting challenge for me, and save her some money. I had wanted to be in business for myself for a long time. I did not want to retire from my current job. I wanted to leave but I did not just want to change jobs and work for another company, yet I did not have a clear business plan for striking out on my own.

How did you make the transition?

At first I thought I knew more about database design than I did. I thought it would be easier than it turned out to be. I started to learn

which is the most widely used. Sybase and Microsoft's SQL Server are also popular choices. You can also look at job ads to see what software expertise is requested most often. When you make a decision, you will need to find out the availability of certification courses in your area.

Scout the terrain. The types of database administration jobs open to you will depend upon the software you choose to specialize in, as well as the needs of businesses in your area. All industries use databases, and DBA jobs are widespread throughout the private, public, and nonprofit sectors. Certain government database jobs will require that you obtain security clearances. In general, the smaller the company, the larger number of hats you will have to wear. You may be not just the database administrator but the general go to IT person, who is also expected to manage network administration and programming, as well as user training. The larger the company, the more specialized the work. In major corporations you may find database design, testing, user training, user support, management,

Oracle on my own but eventually I broke down and took a course. Once I had one database completed, I decided to freelance design Oracle databases. I had a friend in the pharmacy business who needed a database so he became my first client. I do not earn as much as I did before. I sort of took early retirement and try to drum up as much design work as I can.

What are the keys to success in your new career?

Do not be afraid to learn something new. A little humility goes a long way. My wife had to wait a long time for a working database that met all her needs because I was learning as I was designing it. I guess the lesson there is you can practice on family members before you go out and get "real" clients, but try not to inconvenience them too much. Also, you will get better as you get more design practice. And the obvious piece of advice—so obvious that it is often forgotten—is to listen to your clients. Find out what they want their database to do and make it do that, not what you think it should do.

security, and related functions finely parsed out amongst a whole team of IT, business and IT/business hybrid professionals.

Find the path that's right for you. Consider the type of working environment you prefer. Are you a jack-of-all trades type or do you prefer to have a highly specialized role? Do you prefer the business or IT end of the division of labor? Do you want a management position or do you largely want to be left alone in your cubicle? Generally speaking, the higher up you are, the more supervisory and less hands-on your role. Do you have a preferred software package? Would you move for the right job? These are amongst the questions that you should ask yourself as you contemplate this career change.

Go back to school. If you do not possess a relevant degree, you are going to have to return to school in order to make this career change. A background in mathematics, engineering, business, or one of the hard sciences might open doors if you have extensive database experience, but most employers will look for a technical degree and certifications on your résumé. A few lower-level database administrator jobs may be open to you with a two-year associate's degree from a community college or technical institute in computer science, information science, or management information systems (MIS), with certification in particular database software, but most employers will want to see a bachelor's in one of those fields. Some will even look for a master's. A MBA with a concentration in information systems is your ticket to the top level of database administrator jobs. This training would orient more toward the business and management end of things as opposed to the technical side. A master's degree will help you get a supervisory position as a team leader rather than a team member, although experience is also important. Business managers are also often paid more than purely technical staff. A Ph.D. is not normally required, but may be an asset in getting a database development research position.

Essential Gear

Renewing your certification is your passport to travel in this field. Remember that technology evolves rapidly and employers will want to see that your skills are up to date. A bachelor's or even a master's degree that is several years old is not going to assure your employer that you know anything about today's database software and the latest management techniques. Most private database software companies, such as Oracle, offer certification in their products. Obtaining such certification is mandatory. Your employer may pay for continuing education, but you will likely have to obtain the initial certification on your own before you land a job. In fact, a related career option for database administrators is teaching these certification courses.

Landmarks

If you are in your twenties . . . You should have the freshest of skills, which will be an asset on the job market. Employers view younger workers as more tech savvy and, since they can pay them less, tend to favor them. Make sure that you learn database software programs that are widely used to broaden your employment options.

If you are in your thirties or forties . . . Focus on putting together a résumé that shows a good combination of education, experience, and certification. Employers will expect the whole package from you, whereas they might spring for a certification course for a newly minted twentysomething degree candidate in an entry-level position.

If you are in your fifties . . . If you are moving into database management from another IT position, ascertain if you have the business qualifications that a potential employer requires to move up to a managerial position. You want to be certain that opportunities for advancement exist since you might be making a lateral or downward transition to get into your new field.

If you are over sixty . . . You are going to have to fight the assumption that you lack the latest and greatest technical knowledge. At the same time, even flashing certificates from courses is not going to be enough to convince many employers to take on a new IT employee who is over sixty. Not when they can pay a twentysomething half your salary. If you can bring business experience and acumen to the position, you may be able to leap straight into a managerial post, which would be ideal.

Further Resources

Guide to Career Education is a list of online schools and technical institutes offering degrees and certification. Important: Check the marketability of any school's degrees and certificates before giving them a penny of your money. http://www.guidetocareereducation.com/database.html

Filemaker is database software specifically designed for Mac users. It is owned by Apple. Although used primarily by small businesses and individuals, there are some large companies that use it. http://www.file maker.com

Microsoft SQL Server Certification is offered by Microsoft. Receiving the Microsoft Certified Database Administrator (MCDBA) credential will enable you to administer Microsoft SQL Server 2000 databases. http://www.microsoft.com/learning/mcp/mcdba/default.mspx

Oracle is the number one database software used worldwide today. http://www.oracle.com

Computer Systems Analyst

Computer Systems Analyst

Career Compasses

Get your bearings on what it takes to be a successful computer systems analyst.

Relevant knowledge of computer hardware and software (30%)

Organizational skills to keep track of the wiring, coding, licensing, and other details associated with setting up computer systems (20%)

Mathematical skills are generally associated with IT occupations because they indicate an aptitude for coding and related skills (20%)

Ability to manage stress because businesses today are heavily dependent upon the smooth functioning of their IT systems (30%)

Destination: Computer Systems Analyst

Of all the careers in the information technology occupations volume, computer systems analyst is probably the most opaque to outsiders. It is less defined than other careers as the job title can represent various IT-related duties. In the most general sense, computer systems analysts are problem solvers in the IT-verse. Of course, all IT professionals are problem solvers, whether they are dealing with security problems, database issues, network outages, programming glitches, and other challenges in their day-to-day jobs. But computer systems analysts problem solve for a living, starting from the design, development, and installation of IT systems.

There are a number of advantages to entering this field now. The dependence of business on technology is increasing rapidly, and the pace and sophistication of technological innovations ensures that the job market for computer systems analysts will remain robust. In fact, employment opportunities in this field are not only expanding faster than in non-IT fields and but also among IT-related professions. Computer systems analysts are involved from the planning stages in the process of incorporating new technologies into the workplace. Not every new technological development is necessary or appropriate for each company and work environment. Computer systems analysts help companies use technology effectively and efficiently to improve their businesses, guiding them in choosing amongst available options. Since these options are constantly changing, this is a very dynamic field. Computer systems analysts, by the nature of their work, must always be aware of the latest technological developments and updates to existing systems. It will not always be appropriate for a company to adopt each innovation, but the computer systems analyst must always be aware of current and forthcoming options so that his or her employer is never put at a competitive disadvantage by missing out on potential gains in efficiency or cost savings.

Essential Gear

Elaborate on your expertise. There sometimes seems to be a river between the business and IT sides of a company, forded only with great difficulty. In the field of computer systems analysis, there is, instead, a well-trafficked bridge. Unlike in many other IT roles where the IT people work in isolation, using technical skills that could be applicable to a variety of settings, computer systems analysts in a bank are expected to know something about finance.

If they work in a hospital or university, they are required to have some knowledge of health care or educational administration, and so on. Industry-specific knowledge is crucial, so highlight it in your cover letter, not just on your résumé—and be able to talk about it.

The work of a computer systems analyst is quite varied. A good one needs to have an understanding of the business needs of an organization, which makes this a good career choice for someone moving into IT from the business side of things. The computer systems analyst needs to take that knowledge and use it to design or choose a new computer system, including both hardware and software. This work involves close consultation with business managers and end users. This can consist of observation of existing business practices, meetings, surveys, and other forms of collaboration. The IT side of the equation needs to have a clear grasp of the goals that the business side has for the system. The computer systems analyst must also be able to "crunch the numbers" and ascertain the financial viability of technological investments, and assess their probable return. There are many techniques that the computer systems analyst can use in the systems design process, including sampling, cost accounting, data and mathematical modeling, information engineering, and structured analysis. Since the computer systems analyst in this role is choosing the hardware and software that will form the system's infrastructure, you might see the job title listed as "system architect."

After the company's needs are defined, the computer systems analyst might have to develop a system if nothing is on the market that meets the company's specific requirements. In this case, the computer systems analyst may work with a computer programmer or other hardware, software, and network developers to develop a tailor-made solution or modify an existing one. Computer systems analysts who are primarily system developers are often called systems designers. (It is a good idea to look at the duties of IT jobs rather than relying on job titles, since titles are not standardized .) Generally speaking, the larger the company, the more likely it can afford to develop propriety software. Smaller companies are more likely to be financially forced to use out-of-the-box products, although their needs may be idiosyncratic. It takes a resourceful and creative computer systems analyst to provide a small company with a system that meets both their needs and their budget. One way this can be done is to tweak or upgrade existing systems, and stretch the limits of customizability of commercial software.

Once a system is designed, the computer systems analyst cannot turn the development entirely over to programmers. First, detailed specifications must be prepared, including flow charts and process diagrams. Then, once the programmer has made an initial attempt to turn the specifications into a program, the software must be tested and debugged, as well as vetted to ensure that it meets the requirements. Software testing is a career in itself, but computer systems analysts must frequently be involved in it due to the nature of their position. Another job title that covers this type of work is "software quality assurance analyst." If the computer systems analyst does his or her own programming, the job title can become "computer programmer-analyst." This dual role requires an exceptional breadth and depth of skills, but that does not imply that it is unusual. Employers will squeeze as much work out of one employee as they can. Some of the technologies that must be mastered for this role include client-server applications, object-oriented programming languages, databases, Internet-based applications, and multimedia. After the software is rolled out to the end user, the computer systems analyst may be involved in training, observation, and obtaining feedback. If problems are diagnosed (and they always are), the computer systems analyst must find the solutions.

Even if a system meets current needs and functions smoothly, it will need to be periodically re-assessed and updated—more work for the computer systems analyst. The expansion of a company may also create networking challenges. Today, some computer systems analysts may be based in a different country, or even on a different continent from their end users. Telecommuting is increasingly an option, allowing the job to be conducted from most anywhere. Not all companies allow this, but do not hesitate to ask if it is a viable option for a particular employer.

You Are Here

You can begin your journey to computer systems analyzing from a few different locales.

Do you like learning new things? You may know today's accounting software like the back of your hand, but are you prepared to learn tomorrow's? A computer systems analyst is always active in trade organizations and in pursuing continuing education. Your job is not simply to be an expert on today's technology but to have your ear to the ground—or, in this case, your eye to the monitor—and keep abreast of innovations that might improve the image, work environment, profit margin, speed, accuracy, record-keeping, employee satisfaction, or any other aspect of your company. If you are not interested enough in your work to read trade magazines and Web sites, attend conferences, or take continuing education and certification courses, this might not be an appropriate career choice. There are other areas of IT work where it is not crucial

whether each individual is on the cutting edge, so check out some of the other chapters in this volume before you dismiss the idea of an IT career change.

Do you have a head for figures? Mathematical skills are useful in any IT position, but they are crucial for computer systems analysts, who must do a fair amount of number crunching. Every system has costs and benefits which must be assessed to determine the feasibility and return-on-investment for the company. A computer systems analyst who recommends an expensive system is going to have to justify the cost to the business managers who make the spending decisions for the company. Mathematical skills are also necessary for analyzing data and for system configuration. If you have always been good at math and wished that you could put your quantitative skills to use in your career, computer systems analyst may be the job for you.

Navigating the Terrain

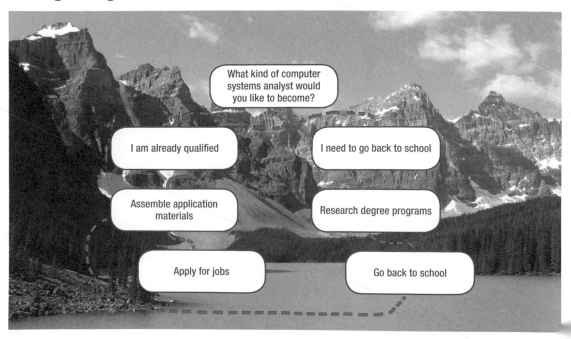

Do you have transferable business experience? As noted in the introduction, computer systems analysts must have a clear grasp of the business needs of the organization. If you have experience on the business side of the industry for which you will now be assessing system needs, your job application will stand out from the others. This is especially important if you are new to IT work and potential employers may have reservations about your IT skills and experience. Also, you may be able to utilize connections you have made in your current career to get your foot in the door, or even to transfer within your present company.

Organizing Your Expedition

Before you set out, know where you are going.

Decide on a destination. Most computer systems analysts specialize in a specific type of computer system. Technology has developed to the point that it is highly task- and industry-specific, so it is not realistic to be a jack-of-all-trades given the level of systems knowledge that a computer systems analyst is expected to possess. Financial and accounting systems are popular choices because all companies, regardless of size or industry, need them: This widens your employment prospects. There are other business systems for areas such as human resources that may be utilized primarily by larger corporations. Other types of systems include those used in scientific and engineering fields. The range of possible employers may be smaller, but the compensation can be higher if you have the specialized knowledge needed for certain technical fields. If you have a background in a specific field, it is an excellent idea to consider becoming a computer systems analyst in it because your familiarity with the industry may bolster your credibility on the job market even if your IT experience is limited.

Scout the terrain. Since the work that broadly falls under the category of computer systems analyst can be so varied, you need to keep two important things in mind during your job hunt. The first point to remember is that computer systems analyst jobs may be listed under many job titles, so broaden your search to include them. Look for the keyword "systems" attached to words other than "analyst," such as "architect," "engineer," "developer," "designer," "programmer," "manager," and others. "Tester" and "trainer" represent related occupations that might interest you. The second point is closely related to the previous one: Under a given job title, the expected job duties and qualifications can vary tremendously. Be certain to read each job description carefully and ascertain if you have the required skills and experience, and if the work appeals to you. The same job with the same job title could differ significantly between two companies in their expectations, workloads and duties.

Essential Gear

Pack your problem-solving skills in your portmanteau. Computer systems analysts are the fairy godparents of the IT world: They turn wishes into reality. Except that this is not always easy or straightforward, given logistical, technological, or budgetary constraints. If you are able to show potential employers that you can analyze problems and think logically about solving them by showcasing examples of this from your past professional experience, you will have a substantial advantage on the job market. Add to this some excellent interpersonal skills to show that you not some antisocial geek who prefers to be uninterrupted in his or her cubicle unless it is for a Mountain Dew delivery, and you will be a strong candidate indeed.

Find the path that's right for you. Your personal road to a career in computer systems analysis will be paved with your prior education, professional experience, interests, location, and talents. A significant crossroad will be determined by whether you come to this career change from an IT background, a business background, or some wholly unrelated profession. Your experience as well as your degrees will be the keys to opening career doors. This profession is a great choice for a career-changer in part because it is recession-proof, dynamic, and provides a variety of tasks. Since there are quite a few jobs out there, you may be less likely to have to move or take on a long commute than for some other jobs, and you are more likely to find a good match for your skills, talents, and interests.

Go back to school. A bachelor's degree in computer science or a related technical field is the rock-bottom minimum requirement. Some jobs will require a master's degree. You cannot expect to find a position in this field with only an associate's degree or a certification course. The balance of IT versus business versus industry-specific education will depend upon the employer. In some cases, those without technical degrees can find work if they have an MBA or a bachelor's degree

Notes from the Field

Arun Patel
Computer systems analyst
Dallas, Texas

What were you doing before you decided to change careers?

I was a computer programmer and LAN [local area network] adminis-trator for an energy company.

Why did you change your career?

I did not really change careers. My job is officially categorized as analyst/programmer.

How did you make the transition?

An opening in the financial services division of my company arose and I was approached. I thought it would bring new challenges and supervi-sory opportunities, so I took it. I later moved to a job with an electronics company, and now I work as a contractor with a federally regulated, PC-based electronic funds transfer system. I gather and validate source

in management information systems (MIS) with technical expertise to bolster it. Likewise, certain employers in technical industries such as science and engineering will look for degrees and experience in their field rather than a general computer science background. All employers will expect applicants to be familiar with the newest technologies. If the ink is dry on your degree, employers will expect to see evidence of continuing education courses. Once you land a job, your employer will usually pay for you to keep your skills up to date, but getting an initial job may depend upon demonstrating that your skills are current.

Landmarks

If you are in your twenties . . . You can start by looking at job ads and getting a sense of what degrees and skills are requested by employers that interest you. Then set out to obtain the relevant degrees. You might *code and I use PC to mainframe SDLC communications with hardware encryption, written in C and 80x86 assembly languages.*

What are the keys to success in your new career?

You must have the ability to learn new languages and master new technologies quickly. You need to be able to do this on whatever propriety systems your current company is using. The more operating systems, languages and DBMSs, hardware and protocols that you know, the better. You need determination to succeed in IT work, as well as a willingness and ability to take advantage of opportunities when they arise, even if they are outside your current work area. I have led projects and conducted system testing whenever asked. Don't be afraid to change jobs and keep pursuing chances to advance your career and learn new technologies. If you can acquire industry-specific knowledge it will help you to move up or move to another company in the same industry, but do not feel limited to one industry as the underlying technology is the same everywhere and you can always adapt.

be able to find a related IT profession, such as software tester, to use to get relevant experience and build your résumé.

If you are in your thirties or forties . . . Concentrate on improving your résumé. If you have a bachelor's, get a master's. If you come from an IT background, get an MBA. If you come from a business or scientific background, get a technical degree or, at the very least, take some IT courses.

If you are in your fifties . . . Work your connections. If you are transferring at this stage of your career, you will need to give a potential employer reason to hire you over younger candidates with freshly minted IT degrees. This is where the people you have met along your career path thus far can come in handy.

If you are over sixty . . . It is the same old story, with a twist. That is, you will still face the stereotypical perception that old timers are not tech savvy, but business experience is valued more highly in this field than in other IT professions. Focus on such experience in your résumé to improve your odds.

Further Resources

Software Engineering Institute is a software engineering research and development center based at Carnegie Mellon University. http://www.sei.cmu.edu

Systems Analysis Websites are conveniently collected on this page maintained by the University of Missouri-St. Louis College of Business Administration. http://www.umsl.edu/~sauterv/analysis/analysis_links.html

Worldwide Institute of Software Architecture is a nonprofit membership organization for software architects that aims to provide information and services to software architects and to promote the profession. http://www.wwisa.org

O*NET Code Connector provides detailed information on computer systems analysis job tasks and how they relate to similar IT occupations. Very good for placing the job in context and comparing it to other IT career options. http://www.onetcodeconnector.org/ccreport/15-1051.00

Computer Software Engineer

Computer Software Engineer

Career Compasses

Get your bearings on what it takes to be a successful computer software engineer.

Relevant knowledge of computer programming, particularly C, C++, and Java (50%)

Organizational skills are needed because building a software program involves many details, none of which can be overlooked (10%)

Mathematical skills are essential for programming as mathematical models and reasoning are used frequently (30%)

Ability to manage stress is critical when you are facing deadlines and must deliver a product that is fully tested and bug-free (10%)

Destination: Computer Software Engineer

Does building flight simulators for the government sound like a cool job? If so, computer software engineering might be the career for you. It might be if you have a bachelor's or master's degree in computer programming or engineering, combined with some relevant work experience. Because the skill set and degree requirements are so specific, this is not the easiest career to enter from a completely different field; however, the upside is that job growth is expected to be rapid in this occupation for at least the next decade. If you can make the switch and enjoy the work, you will be well placed career-wise for the foreseeable future. In order to determine if this is the career for you, let us take a look at what computer software engineers do, and then at what skills they need to perform these duties.

Behind the user-friendly façade of your computer is software and systems that make the computer perform all of the tasks that you ask of it. Whether you are using a drafting software program to make architectural plans, editing a film, or writing a novel, there is a software program geared to that endeavor, designed and developed to run on your computer's operating system, whether that is Windows, Mac, Unix, Linux, or something more obscure. Whereas computer hardware engineers develop the equipment on which the programs will run, computer software engineers design, develop, test, and evaluate software programs for various platforms. Each new piece of software is obsolete almost before it reaches store shelves, because of the need to fix bugs and upgrade its performance with new features—not to mention keeping it compatible with changes to the underlying operating system and other programs with which it interfaces.

Essential Gear

Take along your team spirit. Writing software applications might seem like solitary work, but unless you are a very small independent software engineer working out of your home, every application that you work on will be designed and developed by a team. Technical skills are not sufficient to succeed in this field: you need superb people skills as well. You need to be able to take direction from the lead software engineer, and to be able to communicate effectively with the other members of your team. If you work for a consulting firm, you will work with a variety of client companies and you will need to adapt to different management styles and work environments.

The range of software types that you could design and develop as a computer software engineer is virtually endless, from the mass-produced software used by millions of individuals and businesses around the world (such as games, spreadsheets, databases, word processing programs, and accounting software), to proprietary software used only in specific industries (such as aerospace, geology, financial services, and various health applications and scientific research). If you are interested specifically in designing computer games, there is a chapter on entering that career in Volume 3, *Internet and Media*.

Whether they are designing general use applications or highly specialized utility programs, computer software engineers use the common programming languages C, C++, and Java. Rarely, they may use Fortran or COBOL. Computer software engineers also design the operating systems that run software applications in addition to the software itself, in which case they are sometimes referred to as "computer systems software engineers" to distinguish them from computer applications software engineers. Due to the speed with which job titles change in the computer technology sector, and the fact that most of these relatively new job titles do not have standardized meanings, always look carefully at the position description for every advertisement. Also look for a range of similar job titles rather than just one so as not to miss any potentially suitable vacancies.

Computer software engineers can sometimes engage in related programming tasks, such as designing network distribution systems and compilers, which are required for software to function on a given system. This is akin to translation work, except using mathematical languages instead of words. The work of computer systems software engineers can vary depending upon the type of company and the size of its IT department. At the least, this role encompasses all the work involved in constructing and maintaining the company's computer systems, as well as assessing the need for their expansion or modification. This type of computer software engineer needs to work closely with the business side of the organization for needs assessment. He or she could also be involved in network development and administration of the company's intranets. Although network administrator is technically a job category of its own, the

Essential Gear

Pack an ample supply of patience. Opportunities for advancement abound in computer software engineering, but you do have to pay your dues first. In an entry-level job, you are unlikely to be heavily involved in the software design and development process unless you work for a very small company. You may be assigned software testing at first. Eventually, you can work your way up to a lead design role and eventually to project management. If you bring business skills and experience to your new career, you have a shot at becoming a manager of information systems or even chief information officer. Rather than moving up within one company, you may find that your experience will eventually open doors to different types of computer software engineering work that might present new opportunities and challenges or suit a different stage of your life.

coordination necessary for computers in various departments to communicate with one another falls under the guidance of the computer systems software engineer. It is also possible for this type of computer systems software engineer to work for a systems development company that develops systems customized for individual clients. For this role, the employee would visit the client company to conduct needs assessment and then configure, install, implement, and test a customized system for the client's use. If you have sales or marketing experience, you could be asked to assist the sales team and to provide technical support to the client. Systems security is also partially the responsibility of the computer systems software engineer, although cyber security is a field all its own.

How do computer software engineers decide what software to design and what features it should contain? They start by analyzing the needs of the proposed end user. The next stage is the heart of their work: They design and develop a software program that contains tools to fulfill each of the end-user needs. The software itself is composed or a set of algorithms, or instructions, that tell the computer what to do for each command input by the user. These algorithms have to be converted to a language that a given type of computer can read. Some computer software engineers do this coding themselves but it is often the work of computer programmers. Even if they do not do their own coding, computer software engineers must know operating systems and middleware inside out, otherwise their software will not be functional. Once a prototype program is built, it needs to undergo extensive testing to ensure that it functions as planned, with no errors, and that it complies with the level of technical skills expected of the end user. Adobe Dreamweaver, for example, is a software program that enables users who do not know HTML to build Web pages. The level of technical expertise expected of the end user for Dreamweaver is less than, for example, Adobe Flash, an application from the same company that is geared toward Web designers with programming and Web development skills. Software testing is a field of its own; however, most computer software engineers are involved in testing the software that they create and modify. Software testers are usually part of the software or systems development team. Most IT design and development work is done in teams, so it is important that computer software engineers work well with related technical staff, as well as communicate clearly with the manufacturing and marketing realms of the business. The more integrated and coordinated the different jobs that go into producing the end product, the more useful and coherent that product will be.

You Are Here

You can begin your journey to computer software engineering from a few different locales.

Do you know your ABC's? Well, actually, just your C's will do. Computer software engineers must be fluent in three programming languages, at a minimum: C, C++, and Java. Other, less commonly used languages like COBOL or Fortran can be necessary for certain applications, but spend your time learning the big three unless you are certain that you need a different language for the job you desire. No matter what your background, no potential employer is even going to consider your job application unless it indicates that you know these programming languages.

Do you have a background in an industry that uses proprietary software? Great opportunities for computer software engineers do not only lie with large companies like Microsoft, Apple, Adobe, or Oracle. There are plenty of industries that use proprietary software that is developed in-house or by smaller software companies that cater to a highly specific market. If you are moving into this field, you will need to prove to potential employers that you have the relevant computer science background. That may be tough if you worked in an unrelated field; however, if your field used proprietary software, your expert inside knowledge of that field could partially mitigate a lack of programming experience. Many science- and technology-related fields use proprietary software, as do most branches of engineering and the research side of the health care sector.

Are you female? Computer software engineering is a heavily male-dominated field. If you are female, this gives you an advantage in the job market as you will help companies to meet diversity goals. Also, women are viewed as having an affinity for organization and management that is an asset in this profession. Women also bring a different perspective to the design process that makes a software design team more multi-faceted and improves the usefulness and quality of the final product. If

Navigating the Terrain

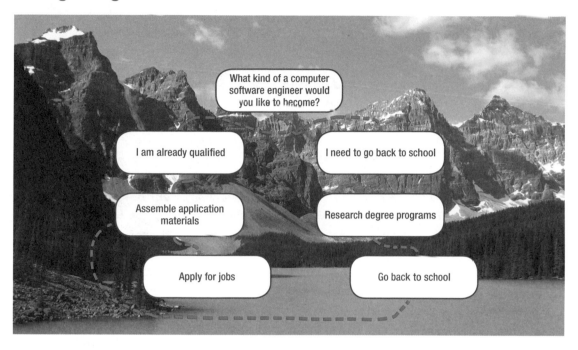

you are a woman with a degree or interest in software engineering and development, then you are going to find this a worthwhile career change that is rich with opportunity and variety of work environments.

Organizing Your Expedition

Before you set out, know where you are going.

Decide on a destination. There are several directions that you can choose amongst to begin your career in computer software engineering. You could design packaged software programs, such as Microsoft Office Suite, Adobe Creative Suite, or Apple's iWork or iLife. You could also design systems software, which is the software that an operating system, such as Mac OSX or Microsoft Windows Vista uses. Finally, you could choose to develop customized applications that are industry or even employer-specific. Each of these options would provide an interest-

Stories from the Field

Bill Atkinson
Computer software engineer
San Diego, California

Bill Atkinson found an unusually successful way to combine his love of photography and his interest in computers and digital technology. He was drawn to nature photography at the tender age of ten, when he received a subscription to the children's magazine Arizona Highways. He cut out nature photographs and taped them to his bedroom walls because he was "nourished and inspired by them." He has spent his life since then bringing his camera to many different natural landscapes, in all seasons and weather, to take photos that can be broad and sweeping or spotlight details with intimate close-up shots. He learned how to become a fine art printmaker, a skill that he still teaches, and later became an expert in digital printing technologies.

Atkinson attended the University of California, San Diego, as an undergraduate, where he met Apple Macintosh developer Jef Raskin, who was one of his professors. He attended graduate school at the University of Washington and then joined the Apple Macintosh development team where he designed and developed several innovative graphics software applications, specifically MacPaint and QuickDraw. He is also responsible for HyperCard, the original hypermedia system. He later left Apple to co-found a start-up company called General Magic that sought to develop handheld communications devices that were

ing and challenging career: your choice will depend upon your interests, skills, and professional background. Another fork in the road involves the choice between working for a software vendor that develops its own branded products, working for an end user company, or hitching your star to a consulting firm that will outsource your talent to various end user companies. Depending upon the company, all three of these options may provide a traditional office environment, a laboratory-like setting, or provide opportunities for telecommuting and working remotely. Most employers will expect a 40-hour workweek, as well as overtime—sometimes extensive—when deadlines are imminent or problems arise.

precursors to the PDA. This company received investment from some major electronics corporations such as Sony, AT&T, Philips, Motorola, and Matsushita. The technologies that General Magic developed were used licensed or sold to such companies as Portico, Icras, Microsoft, and General Motors, for whom it developed OnStar.

MacPaint seems quaint by current software standards, but it was innovative for its time because the graphics generated by it could be used by other applications. We take application internationalization for granted today, but MacPaint was released in 1984 with the original Macintosh computer. This graphics painting software application enabled bitmap-based image editing, producing images that could be cut and pasted into MacWrite documents via the clipboard. QuickDraw was another accomplishment of Atkinson's that remains part of the libraries of OS X today. It is a 2-D graphics library, part of the operating system's Application Programming Interface (API).

Atkinson's success in computer software development has enabled him to focus full-time on his photography in recent years. He has begun polishing and photographing stones and rocks, some of which are featured in his photography book *Within the Stone*. His career is an example of someone who took a hobby that might not have furnished a living but who found a vocation at something closely related and valuable to his avocation. You can read more about Bill Atkinson, listen to interviews with him, and see his photography, on his Web site: http://www.billatkinson.com.

Scout the terrain. Start by scanning the job advertisements in your local classified ads. But remember that most IT jobs are, logically enough, advertised online these days. Your local newspaper may have moved the bulk of its job section online, and there are popular national and international job sites, such as CareerBuilder and Monster, which have extensive IT job listings. Dice is a good choice because it posts IT jobs exclusively. It has jobs cross-referenced by skill set (such as programming language) and location, and it has a special section for green IT jobs. You can search by job title, location, company, or skill. If you find that the jobs for which you have a strong interest and qualifications are not local, you will face the major decision of whether to move in order to facilitate your career change. This is an individual decision that will depend upon the needs of your family as well as your career ambitions, so be sure to find someone that you trust to talk over the pros and cons of making a house move to achieve a career move.

Find the path that's right for you. Congratulations. You have chosen a new career with exceptional growth potential, variety, and excellent employment prospects. The only catch is that you need some specific educational qualifications and skills to get your foot on the first rung of the computer software engineering career ladder. If you are segueing into this career from another IT profession, it is likely that you meet the minimum qualifications. If not, you may position yourself for this career move by taking courses and gaining relevant experience. If you can home in on the qualifications that are required for the jobs you covet by looking at job ads and scheduling informational interviews, you should be able to map a route to get you there in a reasonable time frame.

Go back to school. More good news for potential computer software engineers is found in the area of educational qualifications. Most jobs can be had with a bachelor's degree in computer science or a related technical field like computer information systems or software engineering. Advancement in certain jobs may require a graduate degree, but you may be able to pursue that once you have procured an entry-level job. At some schools, software engineering may be offered as an area of specialization within a computer science degree program. Other relevant areas of specialization include computer security and systems design. A minor in mathematics is a plus for a computer science major because of the use of mathematical modeling, analysis, and algorithms in software engineering.

Landmarks

If you are in your twenties . . . Focus your efforts on obtaining the necessary educational qualifications. For an entry-level computer software engineering job, limited experience will not be an impediment provided that you have the relevant degree and current skills. If your school offers internships, take advantage of those as they provide valuable work experience for your résumé and can help you get an in with potential employers.

If you are in your thirties or forties . . . If you are moving from a very different career, you are going to have to have either a strong computer science educational background or highly relevant experience, preferably both, to impress a potential employer. Go on some informational interviews to get an idea how you rate with the people who are doing the hiring in your proposed field, and what you need to do to be more marketable.

If you are in your fifties . . . At this point in your current career, you are probably beyond an entry-level position, and changing careers may require a step down the career ladder. Be prepared to explain to a potential employer why you are willing to take such a job, and why they should take a chance on you.

If you are over sixty . . . The wealth of jobs in this field makes this career change easier than competing against younger workers in a profession in which jobs are scarce. Yet be prepared to face some age discrimination and retaliate with an aggressive cover letter that addresses the issue of your age directly. Do not let potential employers see the year that you graduated from college on your résumé and wonder why you are applying for the job. Sell yourself in your cover letter and make them look hard for a reason not to hire you.

Further Resources

Virtual Skies Career Radar: Computer Software Engineer is a career description and affinity information Web site maintained by NASA. http://virtualskies.arc.nasa.gov/affinity/M7C1.htm
College Board provides information about pursuing computer software engineering as a college major. http://www.collegeboard.com/csearch/majors_careers/profiles/majors/14.0903.html
Dice is an online IT job classified listing Web site. It typically lists close to 60,000 tech jobs at any given time, and provides IT career news and advice. http://www.dice.com
A Day in the Life—Computer Software Engineer is a YouTube video made by CareerOneStop. http://www.youtube.com/watch?v=CL-vIg4Ivqw

Computer Repair Technician

Computer Repair Technician

Career Compasses

Get your bearings on what it takes to be a successful computer repair technician.

Relevant knowledge of how to troubleshoot and repair computer equipment (40%)

Organizational skills so you do not reformat someone's hard drive when they came in for a stuck CD-ROM drive (20%)

Communication skills to deal effectively and patiently with harried and frustrated customers (20%)

Ability to manage stress should be obvious for any customer service field and needs no further explanation (20%)

Destination: Computer Repair Technician

Computer repair technicians are the unsung heroes of the IT industry. They may receive bursts of effusive gratitude from customers delivered from the "blue screen of death," but it is, in many respects, a thankless job. The upside is that now that the world is run on computers. The world's business systems, financial markets, security, health care systems, and virtually everything else that affects our lives—even driving in our cars— is dependent on them. Computer repair technicians are thus in ever-increasing need. Unfortunately, they will not be laughing all the way to the bank, as this necessary modern service—like most service roles—is undervalued and underpaid. With that caveat in mind, you might want to approach this career change as a temporary stop on your life's professional pathway, perhaps a way to earn money at a time in your life when you value flexibility over salary. But before you make any decisions, let us take a closer look at the specific duties of this important service career.

Broadly speaking, computer repair technicians fix computers and servers, but they may do significantly more than that. Depending upon the employer and work environment, the technician may also be responsible for building and configuring new hardware, as well as installing software programs and keeping them up-to-date. In some settings, computer repair technicians create and maintain computer networks, either setting them up for home users or in a commercial setting.

Essential Gear

Keep your skills up to date. The day after a new version of a popular software program comes out, your phone will be ringing off the hook with people who are having problems installing or using it. The same is true of new computer models and storage devices. There are a lot of people who have to acquire the latest high-tech gadget even though they never learned to program the VCR they got in 1984, and others who are forced by their employers to upgrade software and hardware for their jobs. You always have to be one step ahead of your customers. You may scoff that that is not difficult; just remember to stay perpetually attuned to the latest releases from the major players.

Computer repair technicians can be employed by the public, private, or nonprofit sectors, and they can also be self-employed or work as consultants. The IT departments of large companies may employ computer repair technicians in-house, but repair duty is likely to be assigned to members of the IT staff who also have other responsibilities besides troubleshooting and repair, such as the network or system administrator. Maintenance, upgrading, security, configuration, installation, and even training can also be bundled with repairing equipment as part of the same job. Computer repair technicians also work out of repair service centers. These may be specific to a certain brand of software or hardware, such as a Mac repair center, or they may be general computer servicing operations. Technicians may work on equipment that is brought in to the service center, or they may make house calls (or business calls) to repair equipment on-site. In some cases, technicians in a service center will guide customers over the phone or work remotely on their computers via the Internet. Installing new software or hardware and transferring data are other services that a computer service center may provide. More rarely, technicians in this environment may travel to client's homes or businesses to install hardware or software or set-up networks. Technicians are sometimes able to specialize but the more services a repair center offers, the more versatile the technician needs to be. Retail computer stores also have service departments that employ computer repair technicians. In this case, the technician will service only equipment that is sold by that store, and usually only if it is under warranty. Setting up new equipment and transferring data are likely to be significant parts of the job. Mac stores are one retail employment option, as are large electronics chain stores like Best Buy. You are less likely to be working on older equipment in a retail environment, for better or for worse. The public sector provides plenty of employment opportunities for computer repair technicians, including K–12 public schools and public colleges and universities; hospitals and other health and safety-related environments; law enforcement agencies at the local, state, and federal level; and national security and military departments, which use highly specialized equipment. For some security-related jobs, you may need special training in order to be able to maintain and repair proprietary hardware and software, as well as various levels of government security clearances.

Computer repair technicians can work as consultants who are sub-contracted out by their employers to clients, sometimes on a long-term basis. They can also be self-employed. A self-employed computer repair technician may have more work than he or she can cope with as a full-time job or may do a small amount of tinkering part-time, as a sideline from his or her regular line of work. It is a lot easier to be self-employed in this business if you are not pressured to earn your entire living from it, as business can vary substantially depending upon the economy and the time of year. Technicians usually charge an hourly rate, although some may charge by the job. Most technicians prefer that the client drops off equipment, but some are able to offer pick-up and delivery services, and even recycling of old equipment.

There are no specific degree or certification requirements for computer repair technicians. Some electronics institutes and technical colleges have begun offering certification and associate's degree programs, but most training still takes place on the job. Potential employers will look for mechanical and technical aptitude, evidence of a strong interest in computer software, hardware and networking, and some relevant experience, even if it is relatively informal. There are plenty of opportunities to specialize in this field. Data recovery is one major area of specialization, for obvious reasons. You can also specialize in a Mac or PC environment, in a certain type of server platform or operating system, or in troubleshooting networks, although that is usually part of a system administrator's job and not a stand-alone occupation. You can also concentrate on mobile computing devices or areas like cyber security. You also choose amongst repairing equipment in person, working remotely, or providing technical support over the phone.

A computer repair technician spends much of his or her workday on minor problems, with spyware, viruses, and lost data the most common, but he or she has to be prepared for hardware crashes and re-installing entire operating systems. Repair technicians must be vigilant about backing up data whenever it is possible to do so. Read on to find out if computer repair is the career for which you have been searching.

You Are Here

You can begin your journey to computer repair technician from a few different places.

Do you have mechanical (and electrical) aptitude? Tinkerers are usually born, not made. Did you take apart your childhood clock radio, just to see how it worked? That kind of youthful mechanical curiosity and chutzpah is the harbinger of a "geek" to come. Employers in this field will not be looking for specific degrees or work experience. You will need to convince them in the job interview that you have extensive knowledge of peer-to-peer networks, operating systems, and whatever hardware or software you will be expected to troubleshoot and repair, and then you will have a trial period to prove yourself on the job.

What is on your RSS Feed? Do you keep up with the latest high tech news? If not, you might want to reconsider this career choice. Computer repair technicians must keep up with the latest bug fixes, virus alerts, and other security issues and technology upgrades on their own time. They must be aware of each new video game release before it hits store shelves. They must also network with other techs to share this information on online forums. If you enjoy spending your non-working hours at your computer keeping up with the latest industry news, then you will find this career transition easier.

Are you a personable nerd? Computer repair work is not like computer programming, where you can code quietly in your cubicle all day. In most computer repair positions, you will spend more time face-to-face with your customers than face-to-circuit board with their equipment. You need to have stellar customer service skills, and an ability to translate technical jargon into English. You need massive amounts of patience and sensitivity to the fact that you are dealing with data that most people think of as private. Going inside someone's computer is very intimate, and you need to be respectful of that.

Navigating the Terrain

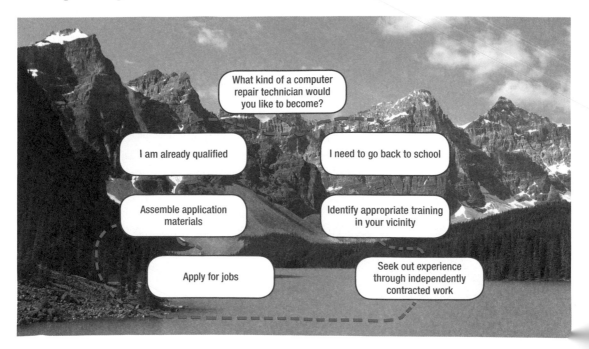

Organizing Your Expedition

Before you set out, know where you are going.

Decide on a destination. You have three basic employment options to decide among: You could be a contractor, be self-employed, or find full-time employment with one company, servicing all of its equipment. The choice depends partially upon what types of jobs are available in your area, your interests, and your need for stability. Obviously, full-time employment is less of a leap of faith than going into business for yourself or even working as a contractor, but those in-house jobs are few and far between. The trend is toward outsourcing more to contractors, so consider a full-time position the Holy Grail if you can find it.

Scout the terrain. If there is a Best Buy anywhere in your vicinity, your first move should be to apply for a Geek Squad position. They have a variety of in-store and field positions, all named in line with their quasi-law enforcement theme. If the Geek Squad does not appeal to you, or is not available in your area, there are plenty of other job search options. Check your local classified ads and online job sites. Most IT job Web sites will list computer repair technician jobs, but not all, since they are considered to be lower level than full-blown IT careers that require a bachelor's or master's in computer science. If all else fails and you cannot find a suitable job in your locale, you can try setting up your own computer repair business. See the linked article at the end of this chapter for inspiration.

Find the path that's right for you. Bear in mind that computer repair technicians are not paid nearly what they are worth. Our technology-dependent economy and society would instantly collapse without computer repair technicians but the glamour and the high pay are reserved for the designers, developers, and administrators of the information superhighway, not the maintenance crew. In May 2006, the median hourly wage was $17.54. That might be considered an acceptable rate of pay for a computer science student looking for a summer job, but it does not provide a living wage for an adult attempting to live independently or support a family. So, as you look into points of entry into this career, carefully consider whether you could live on your new salary and whether the rewards of the job are worth the financial trade-offs.

Notes from the Field

Jim Gregor
Computer repair technician
Hadley, Massachusetts

What were you doing before you decided to change careers?

I had my own business as a Web designer and developer.

Why did you change your career?

The income was not steady enough. I had a lot of small clients who could not afford to pay me as much as I needed to live on to design their sites. I was not willing to move to Boston or some other city to get a job, so I started looking for something around here.

How did you make the transition?

It was not hard. I applied for a job with a local computer repair company and I was hired.

What are the keys to success in your new career?

You have to be nice to the customers. People hate it when the "experts" are condescending to them. I hate it when auto mechanics are condescending to me. When someone has a problem that they never should have had, something stupid that embarrasses them, I always tell them that it happens a lot or it could happen to anyone. Helping your customer save face really goes a long way.

Go back to school. To put it bluntly, this career does not pay enough to make it worthwhile to go back to school exclusively to enter this field. If you are considering entering a degree program in computer science or engineering, then you want to set your sights on one of the other IT careers in this volume. To get a job as a computer repair technician, a potential employer will want to see that you hold at least an associate's degree in a related field, such as electronics. An engineering background can be as useful as a computer science background because computer hardware has mechanical as well as electrical issues. Most employers will offer on-the-job training and will have some sort of apprenticeship set-up where your pay, hours, and responsibilities will increase as you gain experience and competence. There are some certification programs, which may be proprietary to the employer or to a specific brand of software or hardware, that can help you advance, but check with your employer which ones are necessary before randomly investing in one.

Landmarks

If you are in your twenties . . . Consider whether you want to make this a permanent career move or a stopgap. It can be a rewarding job for a natural geek who does this sort of work gratis for friends and neighbors anyway but the pay is low and there are limited opportunities for advancement. So, you might think of this as a temporary career move, a fun job for your twenties.

Essential Gear

Don't forget the main tool of your trade is in your head. Some people utilize the services of a computer repair technician because they are too lazy to read the manual and figure things out for themselves, but most people do not want to spend the money unless they have exhausted all other options and have completely given up on fixing the problem themselves. This means that the simple problems that you will encounter are fewer than you think and the hardware and software problems with which you will be confronted may require some clever diagnostic work. So, pack your thinking cap for this career journey.

If you are in your thirties or forties . . . Use any connections that you have to get your first computer repair technician job. If you are moving in from a radically different field, be prepared to prove to prospective employers that you are a true geek and can repair anything with wires and an LED light.

If you are in your fifties . . . You have an interesting advantage in that computer competence is stereotypically associated with the young, but older customers do not like dealing with snotty young geeks who treat them like clueless old fogies. Play up your ability to relate to your customers and develop a rapport with them.

If you are over sixty . . . Consider hanging your own shingle. There is nothing stopping you from going into business for yourself. That will circumvent any age-related hiring issues that you might face. If you have a reputation for being a dab hand at computer repair, you can build a client base through word-of-mouth.

Further Resources

ComputerRepair.com provides a roundup of the latest industry news. http://www.computerrepair.com

Geek Squad is a computer repair business owned by Best Buy. They set-up and install home networks and theatres and vehicle audio, video and navigation systems as well as repair computer equipment. The Web site includes an article detailing a day in the life of a Geek Squad member. http://www.geeksquad.com

Indeed.com is an online job listings resource that allows you to search by salary, title, company, location, job type, and whether the job is advertised directly by the employer or by a recruiter. It contains extensive computer repair technician job listings. http://www.indeed.com/q-Computer-Repair-Technician-jobs.html

"Computer Repair Technician Jobs—Or Hire Yourself!" is an article on isnare.com that explains how to go into business for yourself as a computer repair technician. http://www.isnare.com/?aid=211570&ca=Career

Cyber Security Specialist

Cyber Security Specialist

Career Compasses

Get your bearings on what it takes to be a successful cyber security specialist.

Relevant knowledge of law enforcement protocols and privacy laws (40%)

Organizational skills to keep track of the many details associated with security—nothing can be overlooked or slip through the cracks in this job (20%)

Mathematical skills are necessary because computer science is essentially a subfield of mathematics (20%)

Ability to manage stress because the consequences of a security breach could be serious (20%)

Destination: Cyber Security Specialist

If an anthropologist in the distant feature were asked to sum up the early twenty-first century, a pithy response would be, "They were an information culture." Information is the currency of the computer age. We make it, store it, access it, modify it, archive it, and retrieve it, instantaneously, all around the world and even from outer space. Unfortunately, some of us also seek to steal it, corrupt it, or destroy it. That is where cyber security comes in. As a cyber security specialist, your job is to keep the reams of information that we produce permanently safe and accessible only to authorized users. It is a dynamic and challenging job because the bad guys who are trying to breach security are working just as fast and as hard as you are working to protect it. New computer viruses are launched every single day and you need to be ready for them. It is not an easy job—let us establish that up front. It is such a necessary job in today's world that employment opportunities are expected to abound for the foreseeable future, but that does not mean it is a sinecure. One significant security breach on your watch and you could be out the door, depending upon whether there is an expectation that you could have prevented it. Depending upon how propriety, important and sensitive the data that you are protecting is, there may be tremendous pressure on you at all times, and you must be able to deal with that on an ongoing basis without burnout in order for this to be a viable career option for you. Before you decide, let us learn a bit more about information security.

Essential Gear

Know your standards. Common cyber security standards exist to make your job easier. They consist of specific security techniques that will help your organization to avoid cyber security attacks. Several accredited bodies provide certification, which can be necessary for obtaining insurance. The most widely used security standard today is ISO/IEC 27002, which was created by the British Standards Institute in 1995. Be sure that you know all parts of this standard backwards and forwards before you go for your first job interview.

Broadly speaking, cyber security specialists protect information, and the systems that house that information, from unauthorized access, disclosure, modification, use, or—worse yet—destruction. This includes preventing the disruption of the processing of information by anything that might shut down parts of the system or render them inoperable even if no data security is breached. There are three components of information security: hardware, software, and communications. The protection of all three is interconnected and falls under the responsibility of the cyber security specialist. There are also three ways that data has to be protected: its confidentiality, integrity, and availability must each be ensured. There are four major aspects of cyber security that the IT professional must know: penetration testing, intrusion detection, incident response, and legal compliance. There are also four major types of malicious programs that can attack a computer system: Trojan horses, which are programs that pretend to do on thing but secretly do something damaging or compromising to your operating system or data; worms, which are capable of replicating themselves and harming multiple programs on a computer; viruses, which can do virtually unlimited damage to data, including destroying it; and malware, which, though hard to detect with antivirus software, usually has more limited destructive capabilities.

Every industry and business that uses computers must take steps to ensure the security of its computer systems, not just the data on them, to keep them functioning smoothly. Protecting the system itself and protecting the data within it are actually two separate tasks, although they are so closely interrelated that it does not usually make sense to speak of them separately. Think of it this way: A security breach that makes customer or client data available to unauthorized users is different than a virus which freezes keyboards or screens and stops work. Every computer in the world is vulnerable to security breaches but information security is particularly crucial for governments in general, and the military in particular. Financial institutions and hospitals also have a lot of extremely sensitive data, although all business are keen to protect their proprietary product information, research, customer data, and financial records. Information might have to be protected for reasons of national security, ethics, competition, or as a legal requirement.

The variety of work environments, data, and equipment used in information storage gives the prospective cyber security specialist a variety of opportunities for specialization in the field. Network security is one of the main areas of concentration, although this work often falls to the network administrator. Securing databases that store information is another possible specialization that you might consider. This is usually one of the duties assigned to the database administrator. Securing applications from malicious attacks by viruses is a never-ending line of work, as is security testing. Securities planning is a field in itself, which involves information systems auditing and designing security systems to meet the needs of a particular business.

At this point you are probably wondering what skills and education you will need to have in order to make this a realistic career move. At a minimum, you will need to know advanced network configuration, including routers and firewalls, and have some basic undergraduate computer science training. You also need to know Cisco systems, IDS, and the major server products from Linux and Microsoft. Mac is a specialize-niche that is less in demand in this field. You will need experience setting up networks, including wireless networks, that use proxy and packet-filtering firewalls, not just a software firewall. You should have set up these networks with several different operating systems. You must also be resourceful and a good researcher; whatever you do not know, you need to be able to find out quickly. You may need some vendor-specific training, such as that offered by Cisco, Microsoft, Novell, Checkpoint, or RSA, but that will vary by job. There are various types of vendor-neutral certifications that might prove useful, including Planet3 Wireless' CWSP, ED-Council's CEH, and Certified Information Systems Security Professional (CISSP). CISSP is the gold standard of cyber security certification. It is the baseline standard for National Security Administration professionals, and it is recognized worldwide. This independent information security certification is controlled by the International Information Systems Security Certification Consortium (ISC) Many employers will also look for Security Certified Program certification. The Department of Defense, for example, requires that certain government IT positions be filled by personnel who possess various types of SCP certifications. SCP offers three certification levels: Security Certified Network Specialist (SCNS), the lowest level, Security Certified Network Professional (SCNP), midlevel certification, and, Security Certified Network Architect (SCNA), the most advanced level.

You Are Here

You can begin your journey to cyber security specialist from a few different places.

Do you work in law enforcement or for the military? Most IT professionals have at least peripheral involvement in cyber security, so a law enforcement or military background is not a prerequisite, but it is useful due to the close connection between cyber security and crime prevention. Most security breaches are also violations of the law, so law enforcement may be involved when hacking occurs. It is also important to remember that methods of protecting data must conform to existing privacy laws. Cyber law is a fast-evolving area of law, as new technologies make new ways of violating privacy or copyrights available. Someone who has a background in law enforcement will stand out as a job candidate from other applicants. If your technical skills and experience are limited, a relevant background such as this could help you get your foot in the door.

Do you like hacking? Yes, you are trying to stop hackers in this job. But to stop them you have to be able to think like them. You need to be able to search for the vulnerabilities in the networks and applications that you protect with the same skill and zeal as a hacker. That means that you spend a fair portion of your work time attempting to hack into your own systems. Like a high-tech version of a cowboy riding the fence line, you need to find all of the weak points before anyone gets in or out. The best qualification for being a cyber security specialist is, ironically, being a first-rate hacker yourself.

Do you have a computer science degree? It is very easy to move into cyber security from another IT profession. In fact, it is part of the job description for many IT roles rather than a distinct position. A potential

Navigating the Terrain

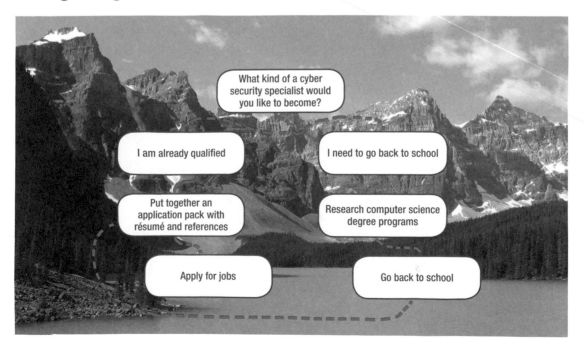

employer is going to want to know that you understand whatever type of system or applications you will be protecting, so related experience is golden. A computer science degree is also expected. If you are moving into this line of work from outside the IT-verse, you are going to have to have that educational qualification on your résumé to even be considered for an entry-level job.

Organizing Your Expedition

Before you set out, know where you are going.

Decide on a destination. The great thing about choosing cyber security as your new career is that the demand for your new skill set is ubiquitous throughout the public and private sectors. You would be hard-pressed to think of a business or government agency that does not use computers today, and, if they use information technology in any way, they need cyber security. So, you can pretty much take your pick as far as industry and whether you want to work for business or government, subject to available job openings and your qualifications. You will also need to decide if you can parlay your current job experience into an entry to your new field. If you work in law enforcement, for the military, with mathematics, engineering, or another IT discipline, then you have a good chance of moving in sideways rather than having to start over with an entry-level position. Corporations are adding a new title to the top of the food chain. Along with CEO and CFO and the now familiar but still recent CIO, we have CSO: Chief Security Officer. If you have had significant management experience, you may be able to segue into a security management role even if you lack a heavy computer science background.

Scout the terrain. Start by looking at job ads. Do not search for the title "cyber security specialist"—that term was coined for this volume, and it does not exist as a job title. Try "information assurance," "security analyst," "intrusion protection specialist," "anti-hacker," and other such titles. If you need additional experience, you might also consider volunteering your time to set up firewalls and antivirus software for local charities. If you live near Washington, D.C., the national government might be a fruitful area to look for cyber security opportunities, starting with the Department of Defense.

Notes from the Field
Kristian Erik Hermansen
Anti-hacker for undisclosed employer
Los Angeles, California

What were you doing before you decided to change careers?

I did not really change careers. I was working for a major entertainment network performing penetration testing as a security engineer. Then a friend recommended that I look into an opportunity in film, which indirectly led to my present work in network security.

Why did you change course?

Actually, my whole team basically got "fired" because of a power struggle between two geographically separate offices. They won.

How did you make the transition?

I saw an ad and it sounded like fun so I applied. I was out of work, so I had nothing to lose. I had relevant experience from working as an information security engineer at the major network, so I got the job easily.

What are the keys to success in your new career?

One key is just getting involved. Didn't someone wise once state that 90 percent of success is just showing up? It is also quite useful to stay on top of new developments in the area of cyber security. It is a rapidly evolving field—we have to stay one step ahead of the bad guys.

Find the path that's right for you. Your first major blowout on the road to becoming a cyber security specialist may occur if you discover that the sort of jobs you aspire to are not available in your locale. Deciding whether to move or settle for a less than ideal position is rarely easy. If you have a family, their needs and preferences must be incorporated into the decision-making process. You must also consider the long-term viability of the job. There is no point in making a move if your new locale will not provide opportunities for advancement or related job prospects in the event of layoffs. Luckily, cyber security is a fairly robust and recession-proof field. When cuts have to be made, security tends to be fairly invulnerable.

Go back to school. As for most of the jobs in this volume, you need at least a bachelor's degree in computer science to have a chance of being seriously considered by potential employers. That might sound like bad news if you are hoping to enter this career from an unrelated previous professional life. But do not despair. This career change is a particularly easy one for other IT professionals to make but it is not impossible for non-IT workers provided you have some patience. You are going to have to get that degree first, but you can do it part-time or on-line whilst you work your current job. You should also go on some informational interviews and see if there are any employers in your area who would take a chance on hiring you partway through your schooling. If you can get an internship, that would get your foot in the door. Regardless of whether you need to return to school, you are going to have to get the certifications alluded to in the first section of this chapter.

Essential Gear

Pack a passion for public service. Terrorists use Internet technology to communicate with one another, move assets, and plan attacks. This has given cyber security an even closer link to national security. Keeping social security and tax records secure is still important, but the focus of government cyber security efforts has shifted to antiterrorism efforts. The flip side of protecting data is accessing it to spy on potential lawbreakers. This brings up many Constitutional privacy concerns that go beyond the scope of this chapter. The point here is that the government is investing in cyber security and will be for the foreseeable future.

Landmarks

If you are in your twenties . . . You have plenty of time to line up the ideal credentials for your dream job. Start with education: If you do not yet have a computer science degree, get one. Then peruse the job ads and tailor yours skills acquisition to the requirements of your ideal position. If you take an entry-level job to start, you will have opportunities for swift advancement.

If you are in your thirties or forties . . . You will need to present an application package to potential employers that oozes competence and that demonstrates both relevant education and practical experience. Look very closely at the requirements of each job ad and explain in your cover letter how you meet each of them. There are a lot of jobs in this field, but there is also a lot of competition, so you need to stand out from the crowd.

If you are in your fifties . . . Think about why you want to make this career change. There must be something related to your current position, background, or hobbies that makes cyber security appealing as your next job. Whatever it is, see if you can exploit it to get your foot in the door. If you have, for example, been responsible for aspects of cyber security at your present job, or if you hack as a hobby, play this up in your applications.

If you are over sixty . . . You need an angle to make this career segue. What experience and skills do you bring to your new line of work? This is where a background in law enforcement or a related IT field can really come in handy. Rather than looking for an entry-level job in your new field, market yourself as an expert consultant.

Further Resources

Cyber Security Specialist is an India-based cyber security firm that provides a full range of cyber security services, including working with law enforcement to solve and prevent cyber crime. http://www.cybersecurity specialist.com/aboutus.html

CERT Coordination Center is an Internet security research institute run out of Carnegie Mellon University's Software Engineering Institute. http://www.cert.org

Bachelor of Cybersecurity: Degree Overview from Education Portal will help you to find out if this is the right degree for you. It provides names of schools with cyber security degree programs. (Be wary of online programs and do not waste your money on them. Most employers do not take them as seriously as genuine brick-and-mortar institutions). http://education-portal.com/articles/Bachelor_of_Cyber_Security:_Degree_Overview.html

SC Magazine is the main industry journal for IT security professionals. http://www.scmagazineus.com

Information Systems Security Association (ISSA) is a professional membership organization for cyber security professionals. It has over 10,000 members in 70 countries. http://www.issa.org

Network
Administrator

Network Administrator

Career Compasses

Get your bearings on what it takes to be a successful network administrator.

Relevant knowledge of network design and configuration (50%)

Organizational skills are very important when you are keeping track of a large computer system (20%)

Ability to manage stress is critical because businesses rely on their computer networks so it can be disastrous if anything goes wrong with them (20%)

Mathematical skills are necessary in all IT work (10%)

Destination: Network Administrator

In the modern business world, we are all connected via our computers, which communicate with each other over networks. It should come as no surprise to you that these networks are not designed, configured, set-up, maintained, and secured by gnomes, but rather by IT professionals called network administrators. Actually, they go by a lot of other names: systems administrator, LAN administrator, network operations analyst, network technician, or information systems administrator, just to name a few. The variety of titles is something to keep in mind when you are looking at job ads.

A network administrator has a lot of responsibilities. He is responsible for maintaining all of the computer hardware involved in a network, as well as installing and upgrading all of the software, whether commercial packages or proprietary programs, that is used by the computers on the network. The network administrator may be involved in the design of the network, and the selection and purchasing of the equipment for it. Obviously, some job details will vary depending upon the type and size of the company. Generally speaking, the larger the company, the bigger the IT department and thus the more finely parsed the roles. In some environments, a network specialist or network analyst will take over design and some security functions, and a network engineer or network technician will be responsible for deployment, but more often these duties fall to the network administrator. All network administrators are involved in configuring the equipment, such as servers, for their network, and thereafter maintaining and monitoring its security and connectivity through the Local Area Network (LAN)/Wide Area Network (WAN) infrastructure. Other IT employees will be involved in network support since it is too large a job for one person, but the network administrator is at the top of the food chain and usually above providing direct user support. All networks require the assignment of network addresses, as well as routing protocols and configuration of a routing table, authentication, and the network's authorization and directory services. Drivers and settings must be adjusted on each individual machine in the network, which can sometimes be done remotely. The network administrator must also see

Essential Gear

Know that the buck stops with you. For routine computer problems, such as lost passwords or other login issues, there should be lower level support personnel on staff—perhaps you in a previous life. For more serious network issues that the help desk has to escalate, most companies should have midlevel network or desktop technicians, although in a smaller company the escalator may rise directly to you. In terms of network support, you are the top tier. On the pro side, this means that you do not have to hassle with the piddly stuff; on the con side, it means that the problems you will be dealing with are the most serious, potentially damaging to the company's productivity and security, and the most urgent. Get used to it.

to the maintenance of the various servers on the network, which can include file servers, VPN gateways, and a variety of types of firewalls and intrusion detection systems. Last but certainly not least, the network administrator is responsible for the security of the network. This is an evolving task, as ways to breach network security as well as ways to keep it more secure are continually being developed. At a minimum, the network administrator must ensure that the network has adequate back-up systems to prevent loss of data, and see that its authentication systems and authorization infrastructure are current and robust. Each device on the network must be assigned a unique IP address, so the network administrator must be an expert in TVP/IP network administration. Troubleshooting and debugging are other important aspects of this exacting work.

That sounds like a wide-range of complex technical tasks, and it is. This is a career for a detail-oriented, logical, organized person with a strong technology background. It is not the easiest profession to break into from an unrelated field. The technical knowledge required is quite specific, and employers will want to see some network experience and may require certification of one sort or another. A network administrator can expect to make at least $50,000 per year, often more. Entry-level network support employees may earn considerably less, but they may also be able to get their job with a two-year technical or trade school degree rather than a full bachelor's. A master's degree may boost your salary and position title, but check the marketability of any master's degree that you are considering before you invest your time and money. Advancement is sometimes difficult without at least a bachelor's degree, but some employers may accept an associate's degree and appropriate certification and experience as sufficient. If you want to know what your employer requires for promotion, ask. Do not waste any time wondering. Also be aware that requirements will vary by employer, so you need to look at each job advertisement carefully and individually.

In the current economy, IT positions are not immune to lay-offs and downsizing. But a business cannot run without a secure network. Both network administrators and network security specialists are going to remain in demand, although employers are expecting fewer employees to carry a larger burden of responsibilities. In the case of network administrators, you may find the support layers underneath you shifting and disappearing so that more tasks fall into your lap, requiring you to work longer hours for the same pay. You may also find that you are hired on a contract basis rather than as a permanent full-time employee. But this is a function of the current economic crisis and not necessarily a long-term trend.

You Are Here

You can begin your journey to network administration from a few different places.

Do you have an IT position currently? If you are already working on the technical side of your business, your employer may pay for you to undertake network administration training if you demonstrate an interest in moving your career in that direction. If you are on the business side, bear in mind that your existing skill set and experience may be less transferable to this job than to some other IT jobs that interact more closely with it. Yes, you will have to work with end users, and ensure that the network meets business needs, but that is not the same level of collaboration needed in roles such as database administrator. Relevant business experience may give you a slight in with some employers, but strong network administration skills are going to land you the job.

Do you have a computer science degree and relevant certification? If you want prospective employers to take your application seriously, you had better have both. This is a career where employers will weigh experience highly. That is, if you have years of network administration experience, they might not care whether you have a computer science degree. But you need the degree if you lack experience and hope to get your foot in the door by securing an entry-level position. See the section below on going back to school for more information on degrees and certification.

Are you willing to take an entry-level position? As noted above, the network administrator is the top authority in charge of a network. He or she may supervise a number of midlevel and entry-level network support personnel, who may conduct basic use support and maintenance functions such as upgrading software, assigning passwords, adding new equipment and users to the network, troubleshooting minor problems,

Navigating the Terrain

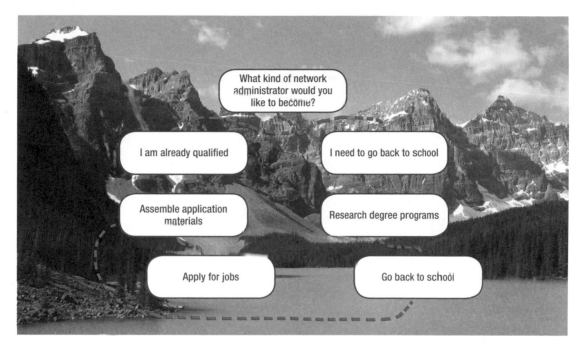

What kind of network administrator would you like to become?

I am already qualified

I need to go back to school

Assemble application materials

Research degree programs

Apply for jobs

Go back to school

and performing data back-ups. Potential employers may expect upwards of five to 10 years of network experience in a network administrator hire. If you are transferring in from another field, it is likely that you do not have that experience, so expect to work your way up.

Organizing Your Expedition

Before you set out, know where you are going.

Decide on a destination. Network administrators are employed by most medium- to large size companies, as well as government agencies, educational institutions, and larger nonprofit organizations. The working environment will vary somewhat based on the type of business you are in and the specific work done by the end users; but, to be honest, backstage looks pretty similar regardless of the type of show going on out front. The biggest difference you will find in work duties is based

Notes from the Field

Caervlevs S. Stator
Network administrator
New York, New York

What were you doing before you decided to change careers?

I was previously a graphic designer, having worked in magazines and book publishing. I also freelanced on the side designing consumer logos, and other media for various clients.

Why did you change your career?

I found that the creative services industry was the first to be affected during an economic downturn. When industries of all sorts cut back on their advertising budgets, graphic designers, art directors, copy editors, and the like are the first to be laid off. Many freelancers (as you know) are affected as well. I experienced downsizing during the economic downturns of 1989 and 1998. In '89 I was an assistant studio manager supervising the layout of three trade medical magazines. The other was after the dotcom bust of '98. Then I was a junior art director of several children and teenage market imprints at Scholastic. In fact, that last downturn affected the impetus of my career. There were no jobs to be had. I was unemployed for two-and-a-half years. I had to move back in with my parents. I then decided not to subject myself any longer to these acute economic forces as a designer. Hence the change in careers.

How did you make the transition?

I attended a technical trade school in order to learn the basics of computer networking for a period of two years. During my attendance, I

upon the size of the company. Think about whether you want to be more hands-on or hold more of a supervisory position. Consider if you want to directly support the end users or whether you would like to be removed from that level of interaction. Then, even if you are certain that you would prefer a larger or smaller company, be open to at least interviewing for jobs in other types of environments. Since you are moving into a new career, you may need to explore to find the right fit. In today's employment environment, longevity is no longer expected and short stints at various employers are no longer quite the negative they once were on a résumé.

managed to get into the school's computer repair shop for six months, and applied the classroom instruction taught. I gained valuable experience, thereby developing various skill sets before graduation. Post graduation, I soon found work as an independent contractor through a headhunting agency. By around 2004, the economy was somewhat picking up. Projects were more forthcoming until landing the current position I have now as a nightshift IT Administrator in 2006.

What are the keys to success in your new career?

The key to transitioning careers is a positive mindset. Such a mindset will fall into place either by desire, or by necessary adaptation. In the real world of IT, many places of employ will require that you be certified according to one's respective skill set. Other places won't require certifications if your résumé reflects the sufficient experience needed for a particular job. I never went beyond my computer technician certification. I am now doing server work at my current job having learned from others. If you are that lucky to come across someone willing to teach you on-the-job server training prior to taking a certification exam, one may then consider taking the exam. Professional experience lends itself to easier study, and the passing of a pursued certification. So far, my boss has not required that I take a server certification exam. If I decide to move on to another IT department, I may need to take it. A good idea is to apply your classroom knowledge as soon as possible, by way of volunteering. Craigslist.com is an excellent source of IT volunteer work (often with pay). Thus, the start of your IT résumé.

Do not change jobs excessively, but do make sure that you find the right position for you.

Scout the terrain. The obvious place to begin your search for a network administrator position is in your local classified job ads. Most IT jobs are advertised online these days, so it makes sense to look at job sites that specialize in high tech jobs, such as Techrepublic.com, as well as general job sites like Monster.com and Indeed.com, which have extensive IT job listings. Be sure to search variations on the job title since IT job titles are not standardized. Network administrator job ads are known for their long and detailed lists of technical skills. Do not be intimidated by this. If you do not know what the acronyms mean, look them up. If you need more information, phone or e-mail the human resources department. Try to schedule a few informational interviews so that you can attain knowledge without feeling too pressured. Ask for a tour of the IT department, if it seems appropriate, to get a sense of your potential new working environment.

Essential Gear

Be a detective in geek's clothing. Wherever there is a network, there will be problems with the network. You will troubleshoot, looking at all the obvious potential reasons for this problem, and none of them will be right. You will try rebooting and debugging and you will begin to pull your hair out and ask for your caffeine via a direct I.V. line. But you will not give up, because you have the soul of a detective, and you will follow each cyber clue until you find the culprit, even if it turns out that someone spilled beer on the server.

Find the path that's right for you. Unlike some other IT professions, it is not necessary to have a background in your employer's industry. Across most fields, network administrators work on the same types of systems, with the same operating systems, server platforms, and software, although there is the rare deviation from these norms in a few highly specialized technical and industrial areas. You do not need to feel constrained by your previous work experience, although you do need to carefully consider your aptitude and reasons for wanting to enter this field. It does offer steady work, but it is work that can seem boring and repetitive if you do not love tinkering with computer connections and configurations. Take the time now to jot down the reasons why you think this is the career for you, refer back to it, and revise it as you gain more knowledge about and experience in your new field.

Go back to school. A bachelor's degree in computer science is a good baseline degree to have on your résumé, but an associate's degree from a technical or trade school, or a bachelor's in mathematics, engineering, or one of the hard sciences is usually fine. That may sound odd since this chapter has emphasized the highly technical nature of this profession. The reason is that any prospective employer is going to be paying much more attention to your certifications than your undergraduate degree. The degree is not sufficient to demonstrate your knowledge of network administration. There are a large number of certificates out there, offered by Microsoft, Linux, Cisco, Citrix, CompTIA, CIW, CWNO, Novell, and TrueSecure. Novell, for example, offers Certified Novell Administrator training courses, and employers using a Novell network operating system will expect anyone they hire from outside to have it as proof of their expertise. Look at job openings in your area before choosing a training course to follow.

Landmarks

If you are in your twenties . . . Potential employers are going to look first at your education and then at your experience. They will want to see a computer science degree with some internship or entry-level work experience with networks. If you have to, volunteer to set up a network for a local charity to get something relevant to put on your résumé.

If you are in your thirties or forties . . . Present to potential employers an appealing mix of educational credentials and experience. Do not expect that IT experience unrelated to networks will be sufficient unless it is in cyber security, computer systems analysis, or database administration in a networked environment.

If you are in your fifties . . . You are going to have to have some closely related work experience for any employer to take a chance on hiring you. Companies depend on their computer networks as their lifeblood, so they are not going to hire someone who has spent years in a different field to ensure their network's functionality and security. In your job search, never forget for a second that the onus is on you to give them a reason to hire you.

If you are over sixty . . . Think about why you want this demanding and often tedious job. Once you have figured it out, write it into your cover letter, because potential employers are going to be wondering the same thing.

Further Resources

The League of Professional System Administrators is a nonprofit membership organization for system administrators. http://lopsa.org

The Network Administrator.com is an equal parts useful and humorous guide to surviving life as a Network Administrator. http://www.thenetworkadministrator.com

NetAdminTools.com is pretty much what it sounds like: a Web site full of back-up and recovery tools, fixes for bugs, and other networking information and tools to help you in your job. http://www.netadmintools.com

Network Administrator Skills Assessment Test from TechRepublic is free and downloadable. It is designed to help employers evaluate applicants but you can take it on your own to gauge your readiness to make this career leap. http://downloads.techrepublic.com.com/abstract.aspx?docid=173659

Systems Engineer

Systems Engineer

Career Compasses

Get your bearings on what it takes to be a successful systems engineer.

Relevant knowledge of the design of complex engineering projects (50%)

Organizational skills to keep track of project specifications and other details (10%)

Mathematical skills are a must for any engineer (30%)

Ability to manage stress is key to surviving deadlines and resolving design dilemmas (10%)

Destination: Systems Engineer

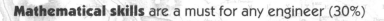

If you would like to engage in highly technical work that is applicable to a wide range of industries, from spacecraft to bridges, from robots to software, from telephones to computer chips, then systems engineering might be the career for you. The diverse projects to which you could apply your skills makes this an appealing career for an engineer who does not want to be pinned down to just one area of specialization. The one feature that all systems engineering projects have in common is complexity. Systems engineering is interdisciplinary by nature and involves the design and management of complex engineering projects. Whatever field an engineering project is in, its coordination, logistics, and control of automated machinery become more challenging with each degree of complexity. A prime example of the type of complex projects managed by systems engineers would be the International Space Station. It requires the input of many designers and developers with diverse skill sets that must all be carefully coordinated. Systems engineers develop the tools and processes that are needed to run complex projects. This unique role means that the career encompasses the divergent skill sets of control engineers on the technical side and project managers for the personnel and business angle. It is an unusual and challenging profession. What unites the projects that a systems engineer oversees is not their ultimate purpose but the fact that they are highly complex, with many steps that are necessary to schedule in a logical fashion, including requirements analysis, modeling, simulation, and stress testing, among many others.

Essential Gear

Pack your leadership skills. A systems engineer is the glue that holds complex engineering projects together. Consider the sort of person whom you would want to lead the team of engineers, architects, health care professionals, scientists, manufacturers, and others who designed, built, and maintain the International Space Station. You need to be that sort of person. Everyone is looking to you to understand every aspect of a project for its entire life cycle. The other team members each are responsible for a specific piece of the whole: ou alone see the big picture. You must have strong leadership skills to play this role effectively.

When you think about choosing an area of concentration within the field of engineering, you probably consider aerospace, electrical, mechanical, civil, and software engineering as likely options. Systems engineering is a bit harder to wrap one's head around as it concerns methods and modeling rather than a particular system, such as an HVAC system that a mechanical engineer would oversee, or a particular item, such as a bridge that a civil engineer would work on. It is not as old as some branches of engineering, having only developed as a distinct discipline in the 1940s. Its evolution was gradual, a result of a need to have methodologies for managing complex engineering projects. Having a project manager oversee a team of engineers and other types of project workers was not sufficient for really complex projects because the whole of the project was much more than the sum of its parts. It was discovered that the management of complexity was a discipline in itself. Various tools have been developed for systems engineers to understand complex engineered systems. These tools include Unified Modeling Language (UML), which is used in the field of software engineering to create abstract graphical models of an object-oriented software system to facilitate its development. It is a method for software engineers to draw blueprints for use in object-oriented software development that provides both structural and behavioral views of the system. Quality Function Deployment (QFD) is another tool for systems engineers that is used to translate customer needs into development targets for a service or product. It is widely used in the military, automobile manufacturing, and software development. A final tool used in software engineering is Integration Definition (IDEF), which is actually an entire family of modeling languages for different purposes including functional modeling, information models, and database design. Like many systems engineering tools, it was originally developed by and for the military—in this case, by the United States Air Force. It is used primarily, but not exclusively, by defense contractors.

Essential Gear

Mix it up. Systems engineering is an odd field because it has fairly rigid educational requirements yet it relies more on practical experience. It is unusual for a systems engineer to study systems engineering as an undergraduate and get a job in this field straightaway. Most systems engineers obtained an undergraduate degree in a traditional engineering discipline, followed it with work experience, and then pursued a graduate degree in systems engineering. The degree is not enough because employers want to see a candidate who is mature, who sees the big picture, and who has proven ability to work with both technical workers and business users. So be sure that your credentials combine education with solid, relevant work experience.

Systems engineering started out as a methodological approach that could be used by any type of engineer who was working on a complex system. Recently, graduate programs have solidified systems engineering into a unique discipline. Students of systems engineering learn how to approach and manage complex engineering projects, whatever engineering subfields may be involved. The process begins with determining and defining the needs of the customer or end user of the product or service that is being developed, including its proposed functionality. The systems engineer documents the customer's requirements in a form that facilitates the design process. The next steps are design synthesis followed by system validation. The focus of the systems engineer is on the totality of the problem at hand, or the complete system life cycle. Charging someone with this holistic perspective keeps anything from being forgotten, at least in theory. The systems engineer combines an understanding of the technical and management sides of engineering and so is uniquely placed to organize every aspect of a complex project.

On the technical side, the systems engineer assesses all available information, defines measures of effectiveness of the final product or service, creates behavioral and structural models, performs trade-off analysis, and creates sequential build and test plans. There are several models that the systems engineer use for the technical processes, such as the waterfall model, in which development is viewed as a sequential process that flows downwards, like a waterfall. The phases in the waterfall model are termed analysis, design, implementation, testing, documentation, evaluation, and maintenance. Another commonly used model is the V-Model. This model also serves the purpose of simplifying the complexities of systems development by graphically representing the mains steps that must be taken in the systems development life cycle, along with the deliverables that correspond to each stage. The V-Model starts with project definition, followed by an implementation timeline, then project testing and integration. The initial project definition phase is subdivided into concept of operations, requirements and architecture, and detailed design. The testing and integration phases include integration, test, and verification; system verification and validation, and operations and maintenance. The verification and validation process is depicted in the center of the "V" to signify its application to all phases of the systems development model. There is a version of the V-Model that is specifically tailored for use in the software development process. It includes verification phases, a coding phase, and a validation phase, each of which are subdivided into activities and steps. The systems engineer must ensure that all of the technical contributors to a project work as a team, with each technical contribution slotted into the correct place in the development process; therefore, the systems engineer must have a good understanding of the nature of the technical work involved, even if it involves diverse technical fields.

In sum, systems engineers work to bridge information gaps between all of the different team members involved in a complex project, such as the end users and operators and the designers and developers. They have many tools at their disposal to accomplish this task, such as optimization, system dynamics, systems analysis, statistical analysis, reliability analysis, decision making, and modeling and simulation. Systems engineering is a relatively new and inherently interdisciplinary subfield in engineering. Read on to discover how you can enter this unusual field.

You Are Here

You can begin your journey to systems engineering from a few different places.

Do you have an engineering degree? Although the type of engineering degree needed may vary by employer (and type of complex product or service), the minimum qualification for any systems engineering job is going to be a B.S. in an engineering field, with an M.S. often required. Aerospace/aeronautical, mechanical, or electrical engineering are all plausible degrees for systems engineering. For software engineering specifically, you will need a computer science or computer engineering degree.

Do you have project management experience? A systems engineer is a glorified project manager. You must be familiar with all phases of project management, and have had responsibility for managing large and complex projects to have a hope of getting a systems engineering job. In some cases, the project manager coordinates the interaction of the project stakeholders but has little input into the decision-making processes. A systems engineer has to have additional skills that go far beyond traditional project management. Just like a complex system is more than the sum of its parts, a systems engineer is more than a project manager who can manage large and complex projects. The systems engineer actually takes the customer requirements and leads a logical sequence of activities and decisions that will result in the operational need being transformed into new system performance parameters.

Are you detail-oriented? If you are truly acquainted with your new career choice, that question should elicit a chuckle. There are certainly

Navigating the Terrain

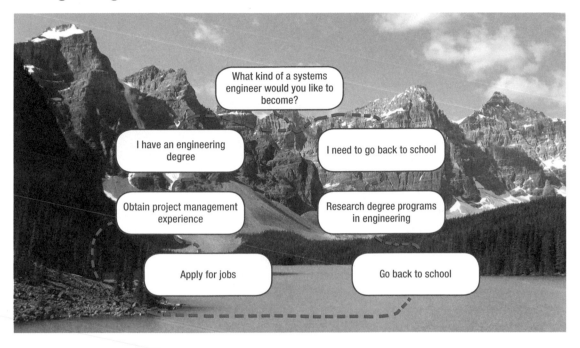

What kind of a systems engineer would you like to become?

I have an engineering degree

I need to go back to school

Obtain project management experience

Research degree programs in engineering

Apply for jobs

Go back to school

other jobs that require as much attention to detail—microsurgeon comes to mind—but that does not change the fact that being detail-oriented is crucial for a systems engineer. After all, the whole point of the role is to ensure that no detail is forgotten or conducted out of order in a long, complex process. It is like choreographing an enormous ballet production except that at the end of it you end up with a rocket or a bridge instead of *Swan Lake*.

Organizing Your Expedition

Before you set out, know where you are going.

Decide on a destination. It should be clear right now that systems engineering is only a career option for someone who is already an engineer. If you are thinking of segueing into this field from another discipline, your first decision will be picking a specialization within engineering and going back to school for a degree in electrical, mechanical, aerospace/

Notes from the Field

Eugene Sobinski
Systems engineer
Elkhart, Indiana

What were you doing before you decided to change careers?

I was a mechanical engineer for a construction company that has government contracts for large municipal projects, such as bridges and tunnels and sewage and drainage systems.

Why did you change your career?

I had been a project manager for many years and I was seeking to expand that role.

How did you make the transition?

As I gained project management experience, I got to manage larger projects. At some point, the project management tools that you need change, for projects over a certain size. I did some research and found

aeronautic, civil, or software engineering. So consider carefully which engineering discipline appeals to you are your base or foundation for your career in systems engineering. If you already have an engineering degree, then you will need to consider if your previous work experience will help you get a particular type of systems engineering job. Employers usually want to see five to 10 years' relevant experience in a systems engineering candidate. So, your choice of a destination is really going to be limited by your education and previous experience. If you are reading this volume because you want to change careers, it may be disheartening to learn that the educational and experiential requirements for systems engineering are so specific, but do not let that discourage you. Pick where you want to end up and take the concrete steps necessary to get there, as you would for any career change. Just be aware that, depending upon how far removed your previous professional life is from systems engineering, it may take you a bit longer.

Scout the terrain. Systems engineering jobs are advertised everywhere that other engineering jobs are posted, but they tend to be concentrated a master's in systems engineering that I could do part-time around my current job. I even persuaded my employer to cover the cost. The catch was that I felt obligated to continue working there and not seek other opportunities, but that has been fine since I love my job.

What are the keys to success in your new career?

Engineers are not known for their communication skills. A systems engineer is in what you might call a customer-service area of engineering. You need to have well-developed verbal and written skills to communicate with clients and the business team of the project. My undergraduate degree—so long ago now I barely remember it—was very technical. The systems engineering program taught me about finances, economics and cost estimation, as well as organizational leadership and decision-making in the face of uncertainty and risk. I had picked some of that up along the way, but this program formalized it. I already knew a lot about modeling and simulation, but this course put those skills in a systems design/architecture framework.

in the aerospace/aeronautics industries and within the government. Various branches of the military hire systems engineers, as does the CIA. The main Web site that you want to visit in your job search is SystemsEngineerJobs.com (http://www.systemsengineerjobs.com), which posts job opening for systems engineers and other IT professionals. You can post your résumé as well as search posted jobs by location, job title, company or key word, and avail yourself of their career resources.

Find the path that's right for you. There are a number of fields that are similar to systems engineering that you might want to consider as possible career options either on the path to a systems engineering job or as a substitute that may more closely match your skills and experience. These fields include: cognitive systems engineering, configuration management, control engineering, industrial engineering, interface design, operations research, reliability engineering, performance engineering, safety engineering, security engineering, and software engineering. Look these careers up on the Internet and read more about them, then scour job ads online. If you qualify for one of these jobs, you may be able to get your employer to pay for systems engineering professional certification that will enable you to move into your desired career.

Go back to school. The thinking within the field of engineering is that systems engineers need both training and practical experience in one of the traditional engineering disciplines before embarking upon a career in systems engineering. Thus, you are not likely to find an undergraduate major in systems engineering. If you have an undergraduate engineering degree, then you might look into certification or graduate courses in systems engineering. There are a growing number of universities with strong engineering programs that offer graduate courses in systems engineering. The International Council on Systems Engineering, a trade organization that you will probably want to join, offers four levels of systems engineering professional certification. Their Web site helps you find which certification is right for you, and where and how to get it. You must have an acceptable technical undergraduate degree to be eligible for the certification, although it does not have to be in engineering. There are a few hard science disciplines, such as computer science, mathematics, and physics, that they will accept. The INCOSE Web site lists which degrees are acceptable. As always, find out what your prospective employer requires before spending money or time on any coursework or certifications.

Landmarks

If you are in your twenties . . . You should focus on obtaining an engineering or hard sciences degree and getting an entry-level job in your engineering discipline. Make it clear in your cover letter and on your résumé that you have a particular interest in pursuing systems engineering and seek out employers that use systems engineers so you can obtain relevant experience.

If you are in your thirties or forties . . . If you are currently working as an engineer of one sort of another, let your employer know that you are interested in systems engineering. You may be able to arrange an internal transfer or at least be assigned to complex projects so that you can work with systems engineers. Your employer might also pay for you to take continuing education or certification courses.

If you are in your fifties . . . The advice given above hold true for you as well. If you are an engineer, you may not have to change employers to move into systems engineering. If you must change employers, or desire to, look carefully at job ads to see how close your experience is to the qualifications sought and try to remedy any gaps.

If you are over sixty . . . You are in luck because experience is valued highly in the field of systems engineering. Also, for INCOSE certification, systems engineers with over 15 years experience can obtain certification even if they lack an acceptable undergraduate degree. Look for an employer who will appreciate your experience.

Further Resources

International Council on Systems Engineering (INCOSE) is a non-profit membership organization for systems engineers. Site includes a job bank as well as education information. http://www.incose.org

Microsoft Certified Systems Engineer (MCSE) provides information on how and why you might want to gain this certification, which is available on Windows Server 2003 or Windows 2000. http://www.microsoft.com/learning/mcp/mcse/default.mspx

What is Systems Engineering?: A Consensus of Senior Systems Engineers is a useful article on the University of Arizona Web site that defines and summarizes this interdisciplinary field. http://www.sie.arizona.edu/sysengr/whatis/whatis.html

Control Engineering Virtual Library is based at the Department of Engineering at the University of Cambridge. It contains links to systems engineering resources around the world. http://www-control.eng.cam.ac.uk/extras/Virtual_Library/Control_VL.html

Forensic Computing Specialist

Forensic Computing Specialist

Career Compasses

Get your bearings on what it takes to be a successful forensic computing specialist.

Relevant knowledge of rules of evidence (40%)

Organizational skills to keep track of your cases and suspects (20%)

Caring about the personal property and privacy of the owners of the computers you are invading (30%)

Ability to manage stress is always essential in law enforcement (10%)

Destination: Forensic Computing Specialist

It is a safe bet that you are reading this chapter because a television show like *CSI* has given you a fascination with forensic science and you feel compelled to pursue a career in this field, even if you had never previously considered working in law enforcement. The detective work used in gathering digital evidence for use in criminal and civil cases is appealing to computer aficionados in a way that the old investigate tools such as handwriting analysis and fingerprinting may not have been. It is high-tech detective work that seems more like playing a dynamic video game than actual toil. This can be an exciting career that will enable you to combine your technical skills with a fantasy of being a modern-day Sherlock Holmes, but it is also a job with strict qualifications and a need for maturity, confidentiality, and attention to detail. Let us begin by examining what computer forensics is and then consider what forensic computing specialists do in their jobs.

Forensic computing specialists work in an area of law enforcement known as forensic science. Forensics refers to evidence collecting in criminal and, in some cases, civil procedures. It involves scientifically analyzing crime scenes, people, and objects to collect evidence that may help prove guilt or innocence in a court of law or affect a settlement amount in a civil case. The methods of scientific analysis that are employed vary according to appropriateness, cost, and available technology. Criminals today are sometimes convicted or exonerated on the basis of evidence, such as DNA, that was not available even a few years ago. Digital or computer forensics is a relatively new branch of forensics that involves analyzing computer storage devices, such as hard drives and disks or CD-ROMs, for evidence of illegal activities that can be used in a court proceeding. Before criminals had access to computers, cybercrime was impossible. Now it is growing more common by the day, bringing with it an increased need for forensic computing experts to ferret out terroristic plans, blackmail, pedophilia, sexual harassment, financial fraud, illegal

Essential Gear

Do not forget to pack your compassion. In the twenty-first century, our computers have become almost like additional appendages. We do not know how we lived without them since we record almost every aspect of our lives in them. Every unflattering picture we have taken, every love letter written but never sent, every Web search to look up some medical symptom we are too embarrassed to ask about or to find out whatever happened to the boy or girl we had a crush on in sixth grade, our attempt at a novel, and many other personal things are all preserved on our computers. When a stranger looks at it, they are gaining access to a part of our lives that we never intended to be made public. Leaving aside the concept of innocent until proven guilty, it is important to be sensitive to the privacy and humanity of the person whose computer you are raiding. Not every aspect of their life is going to be relevant to the case, and they are going to want their computer back, unscathed, when the case is over.

spying, industrial espionage, and intellectual property theft and other forms of copyright infringement. Some types of crimes are committed with the use of computers, such as hacking or distributing child pornography. Other crimes are not committed with a computer, but the computer data storage equipment of the accused may contain useful information and evidence even if the user thinks that he or she never saved the information or has deleted the information and defragmented and reformatted the hard drive or other storage device. Forensic computing specialists also work with cyber security specialists to fix security holes in computer systems by attempting to hack into them and exposing vulnerabilities.

These cybercops, or "digital detectives" as they are sometimes known, have quite a few tools at their disposal in their search for digital fingerprints, such as e-mail converters, password crackers, and a variety of software applications like EnCase and Forensic Toolkit (FTK) that have been developed just for this field. They must be experts at retrieving information that has been deleted, hidden, encrypted, or otherwise made deliberately difficult to find and analyze. There are many steps in the process of building a case using digital forensics, and they must be followed with careful attention to relevant laws or the evidence will not be admissible in court.

The forensic computing specialist's work usually starts with determining if a given computer or related electronic storage device might contain relevant information. At this point, the investigator does not necessarily have free rein to hack into the system. He or she must respond to a particular mandate by using his or her software programs and special hacking methods to retrieve and examine specific types of information called for in the investigation. He or she must next prepare reports on what has been found, according to specific protocols, and may have to provide expert testimony.

To ensure that no evidence is destroyed during the investigation, the forensic computing specialist will first make a copy of the drive that is being examined. This is a special type of copy, an actual mirror image of the original, that can only be made using specialized forensics tools and software: It a bit-by-bit image, not a mere copy of the data. This is a critical step because the investigator must examine the computer exactly as the accused left it, and just turning on a computer alters some of its data. Next the investigator uses hash codes to assure chain of custody. In lay terms, that means that a large number is computed mathematically and assigned to each file on the drive. If a file is altered in the tiniest fashion, its hash code will change. Hash codes from the image and the original can then be compared to ensure that the examination process, which is done on the image to leave the original untouched, does not alter the data being examined. It is one of the basic features of computer operation that makes most forensic computing work possible. When a file is deleted, it is no longer visible to the user but it remains on the computer until that file space is actually overwritten with new data. Until this time, it can be retrieved by someone who is intimately acquainted with the computer's operating system and has special tools to access it. Even if the disk space used by the deleted files has been partially overwritten with new data, the computer forensics specialist can often retrieve parts of it. This is true even if the user has defragmented or reformatted his or her drive, because rebuilding a file system does not remove old information. The same principle applies to data

Essential Gear

Get over the cool factor. Television shows and movies have a way of glamorizing careers that, in real life, are much more mundane and routinized. This is not to argue that computer forensics is a boring career; far from it, but it does have its share of repetition and stultification. For better or worse, most cases that require digital evidence involve financial fraud, not physical violence. You are much more likely to be sifting through financial records on someone's home computer to find evidence of hidden financial assets that can be used in a divorce case than uncovering the client list of a Washington, D.C., madam or busting an international child porn ring. Those cases do happen, but not everyday, and you will be sorely disappointed if you go into your job expecting it to be as action-packed as it looks on television.

that the user thinks he or she has not saved. The computer stores this data temporarily and invisibly to the user, until it is actually overwritten with subsequent data. Forensic computing specialists know how to access this temporary storage space and retrieve the information hidden there. The way that browsers use cookies to track a user's Internet activity makes it easy for forensics investigators to find out what Web sites a user has visited. Additionally, many software programs retain metadata about each file created with that program. The metadata contains the history of that file from its creation, including a record of each time the file was accessed or modified. As you might imagine, this information can be useful in an investigation.

The work of forensic computing specialists is exacting, extremely detail oriented, and sensitive for numerous reasons. The forensic computing specialist must work closely with law enforcement officials to ensure that all legalities, such as Federal Rules of Evidence, are upheld in the examination process, and ensure the integrity of the evidence by making a disk image, examining the image, and providing a verifiable chain of custody. It is crucial that no one but a professional forensic computing specialist touches a computer once it becomes suspect. If you think this is the career for you, read on for more information on how to make the switch into this growing offspring of the IT and law enforcement fields.

You Are Here

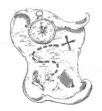

You can begin your journey to forensic computing specializing from a few different locales.

Do you have law enforcement or military experience? Some computer forensics specialists now work in the private sector, for law firms or consulting companies, but most are employed by federal, state, or local law enforcement. If you are already employed in some branch of law enforcement, it will be easier to more into computer forensics work. You may be able to request a transfer and you may be eligible for vacancies that are only advertised internally. If you are not employed in law enforcement, you will have to meet all of the other qualifications for law enforcement jobs aside from the specific technical skills needed for computer forensics work, such as passing a background check and the civil service exam.

Do you have stellar computer skills? Remember that a computer forensics specialist is a glorified hacker. You need to know the ins and outs of every type of computer operating system, including how to get into every type of computer storage device and through every form of password protection. You must know as many programming languages as possible, as well as numerous software applications, software drivers, networking, routing, communication protocols, security, cryptology, reverse software engineering, and so on. This is a job for a dedicated and skillful hacker. If that describes you, you could be paid to hack in a somewhat ethical matter instead of using your skills maliciously.

Have you worked in cyber security? Cyber security is a related career. The cyber security specialist is trying to keep hackers, viruses, and other malware out of individual computers and computer networks, and to preserve data by preventing its loss or corruption. A cyber security specialist may also be charged with permanently erasing sensitive data so that it does not fall into the wrong hands. The skills needed for this career bear a strong similarity to those needed in computer forensics work, so a background in cyber security could open some career doors for you.

Organizing Your Expedition

Before you set out, know where you are going.

Decide on a destination. Forensic computing specialists can specialize in several different areas. Some provide evidence, working with law enforcement agencies on computer-related crimes. It is critical for this specialty that you know the legalities related to search and seizure so that the evidence you collect stands up in court. You must also know standard techniques for collecting and preserving evidence. Some forensic computing specialists do work that is more like cyber security, such as securing computer networks at financial institutions. You will need industry-specific knowledge for this work, such as a background in finance. Forensic computing specialists are also hired to do investigative work by federal, state, and local law enforcement agencies, and private sector companies, such as credit card and insurance companies and law firms. There are consulting companies that send forensic computing specialists out to clients, but many forensic computing specialists are self-employed.

Scout the terrain. You will want to start your search for a computer forensics job by looking at job listings in your local classifieds and online. Many companies today use recruiting agents and employment staffing firms to screen candidates, so you may find yourself dealing with them rather than directly with potential employers. Most computer forensics jobs are with law enforcement agencies or military or government intelligence agencies, each of which maintains their own recruiting Web sites. However, a general place to start looking is with USA Jobs (http://www.

Navigating the Terrain

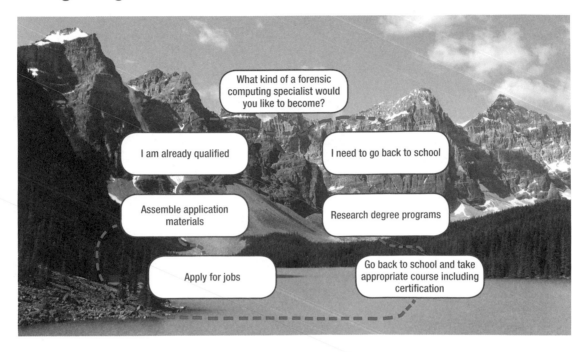

usajobs.opm.gov). Major online job sites such as Dice.com and Monster.com will also have many listings in this field. Be sure to use a variety of keywords in your searches as job titles vary. Try "digital forensics" as well as "computer forensics." Some titles are really stretching it, such as "Vulnerability Security Research Engineer," so keep a sharp lookout for strange job titles on your searches.

Find the path that's right for you. You have choices about where you want to work in the field of computer forensics, but every option is not going to be equally appealing to you or equally possible. Working for the military is going to be quite a different experience than working as an independent consultant, just as working for a law firm is going to be quite a different environment from working for a municipal police force. Some of these jobs are going to require military or law enforcement training or security clearances that not everyone can obtain. Just do your research and you will find which computer forensics job is the right fit for your skills, talents, interests, and abilities.

Notes from the Field

Paul Renzulli
Computer forensics investigator
Huntington, New York

What were you doing before you decided to change careers?

I was begging to get into an IT position, I tried several times but with no formal schooling and no certifications I wasn't very marketable in the post dotcom era. I worked for USAA as a home and auto insurance agent. It was a call center job. Then I worked at University of Phoenix as an enrollment counselor for the BSN, MSN, BSHA, and MSHA programs.

Why did you change your career?

Computers had been a hobby of mine for about 10 years prior to getting into EDD and then forensics. The two are synonymous. My passion was to get into an IT position. I went to school and went through the CCNA and CCNP programs, but didn't get certified. I knew halfway through the CCNP program that networking wasn't my thing. Watch-

Go back to school. Like most trendy new fields, computer forensics is rife with educational scams. Real colleges and universities are offering courses in computer forensics, and taking these courses as part of a computer science or criminal justice bachelor of sciences degree will indeed help you to get a job in this field. There are also certificates and degree courses from technical institutes and online universities that are accredited by no one but themselves. Think for a minute of the chain of events here: 1) popular television show raises profile of career, makes it seem exciting; 2) fly-by-night operators see dollar signs, cash in by offering "certification" in this new field; 3) employers do what they always do: hire people who can prove they know what they are doing, and ignore meaningless certificates they have never heard of. Do not be taken in by scams. A forensic computing specialist needs to have strong technical computer skills combined with law enforcement knowledge. You do not need a computer forensics degree or certificate per se to acquire these skill sets. If you need to bolster your skills, there may very well be a ing 1's and 0's go across a wire wasn't as thrilling as *Electronic Data Discovery* (sarcasm). After 6 months of working at IPRO I was hooked. EDD can put anyone to sleep just by describing what it is, but the passion to find every little detail about every little document is where it is at. That is when I got the fever. But to answer your question in full, it was really partly out of trying to find an IT related job, and the necessity to keep the lights on.

How did you make the transition?

I applied to IPRO Tech and got involved in Electronic Data Discovery as a System Engineer. After 2 years I worked for ImageNet where I was the Senior Production Manager. We would get hard drives in form the clients and have to forensically copy them. That is how I got my start.

What are the keys to success in your new career?

Always looking at new technology, keeping up on the Operating Systems, and applications. I mostly use my talents for EDD these days for what I do. But I have to know how the forensics work to be able to speak to EDD.

legitimate program that would benefit you in the job market, but investigate their placement success and ask employers what they are looking for before you invest your time or money.

Landmarks

If you are in your twenties . . . Your plan of action should be majoring/minoring in some combination of criminal justice and computer forensics, then seeking a job in law enforcement. Plan now for taking the civil service exam and looking at which agencies have available openings that could lead to computer forensics work.

If you are in your thirties or forties . . . You need to make a move if you would like to work in law enforcement because your time is running out. If you do not have a relevant degree, seek out a certificate in computer forensics, and look for related jobs out side of law enforcement agencies, too, such as with law firms or consulting companies. You might consider cyber security as an alternative or interim career option.

If you are in your fifties . . . Your options depend upon what you are doing now. If you are already involved in law enforcement, you can request a transfer or apply for internally advertised positions in computer forensics. If you are not currently employed in law enforcement, it may be too late for you to get a foot in that door, but you could work for private consulting companies and law firms.

If you are over sixty . . . You face some unique challenges in making this career transition. Most federal, state, and local law enforcement agencies have maximum entry and retirement ages. If you are already employed in law enforcement and you are looking to transfer to computer forensics rather than retire, you may be able to convince your employer that you are needed and merit an exception.

Further Resources

New Technologies, Inc. (NTI) is a major computer forensics conglomerate, which trains computer forensics experts, supplies forensics equipment, and provides expert computer forensics services and consulting. http://www.forensics-intl.com/index.html

Computer Forensics 101 is a guide to what computer forensics is and how it can be used by law enforcement. http://www.expertlaw.com/library/forensic_evidence/computer_forensics_101.html

Forensic Association of Computer Technologists (FACT) is a nonprofit organization whose mission is to train law enforcement in the use of computer forensics. Their motto is, "Take a byte out of crime." http://www.byteoutofcrime.org

International High Technology Crime Investigation Association (HTCIA) is an organization dedicated to promoting the exchange of information, experience, ideas and knowledge related to high tech crime investigation and security. http://www.htcia.org

Appendix A

Going Solo: Starting Your Own Business

Starting your own business can be very rewarding—not only in terms of potential financial success, but also in the pleasure derived from building something from the ground up, contributing to the community, being your own boss, and feeling reasonably in control of your fate. However, business ownership carries its own obligations—both in terms of long hours of hard work and new financial and legal responsibilities. If you succeed in growing your business, your responsibilities only increase. Many new business owners come in expecting freedom only to find themselves chained tighter to their desks than ever before. Still, many business owners find greater satisfaction in their career paths than do workers employed by others.

The Internet has also changed the playing field for small business owners, making it easier than ever before to strike out on your own. While small mom-and-pop businesses such as hairdressers and grocery stores have always been part of the economic landscape, the Internet has made reaching and marketing to a niche easier and more profitable. This has made possible a boom in *microbusinesses*. Generally, a microbusiness is considered to have under ten employees. A microbusiness is also sometimes called a *SoHo* for "small office/home office."

The following appendix is intended to explain, in general terms, the steps in launching a small business, no matter whether it is selling your Web-design services or opening a pizzeria with business partners. It will also point out some of the things you will need to bear in mind. Remember also that the particular obligations of your municipality, state, province, or country may vary, and that this is by no means a substitute for doing your own legwork. Further suggested reading is listed at the end.

Crafting a Business Plan

It has often been said that success is 1 percent inspiration and 99 percent perspiration. However, the interface between the two can often be hard to achieve. The first step to taking your idea and making it reality is constructing a viable *business plan*. The purpose of a business plan is to think things all the way through, to make sure your ideas really are profitable, and to figure out the "who, what, when, where, why, and how" of your business. It fills in the details for three areas: your goals, why you think they are attainable, and how you plan to get to there. "You need to know where you're going before you take that first step," says Drew Curtis, successful Internet entrepreneur and founder of the popular newsfilter Fark.com.

Take care in writing your business plan. Generally, these documents contain several parts: An *executive summary* stating the essence of the plan; a *market summary* explaining how a need exists for the product and service you will supply and giving an idea of potential profitability by comparing your business to similar organizations; a *company description* which includes your products and services, why you think your organization will succeed, and any special advantages you have, as well as a description of *organization* and *management*; and your *marketing and sales strategy*. This last item should include market highlights and demographic information and trends that relate to your proposal. Also include a *funding request* for the amount of start-up capital you will need. This is supported by a section on *financials*, or the sort of cash flow you can expect, based on market analysis, projection, and comparison with existing companies. Other needed information, such as personal financial history, résumés, legal documents, or pictures of your product, can be placed in *appendices*.

Use your business plan to get an idea of how much startup money is necessary and to discipline your thinking and challenge your preconceived notions before you develop your cash flow. The business plan will tell you how long it will take before you turn a profit, which in turn is linked to how long it will before you will be able to pay back investors or a bank loan—which is something that anyone supplying you with money will want to know. Even if you are planning to subside on grants or you are not planning on investment or even starting a for-profit company, the discipline imposed by the business plan is still the first step to organizing your venture.

A business plan also gives you a realistic view of your personal financial obligations. How long can you afford to live without regular income? How are you going to afford medical insurance? When will your business begin turning a profit? How much of a profit? Will you need to reinvest your profits in the business, or can you begin living off of them? Proper planning is key to success in any venture.

A final note on business plans: Take into account realistic expected profit minus realistic costs. Many small business owners begin by underestimating start-ups and variable costs (such as electricity bills), and then underpricing their product. This effectively paints them into a corner from which it is hard to make a profit. Allow for realistic market conditions on both the supply and the demand side.

Partnering Up

You should think long and hard about the decision to go into business with a partner (or partners). Whereas other people can bring needed capital, expertise, and labor to a business, they can also be liabilities. The questions you need to ask yourself are:

☞ Will this person be a full and equal partner? In other words, are they able to carry their own weight? Make a full and fair assessment of your potential partner's personality. Going into business with someone who lacks a work ethic, or prefers giving directions to working in the trenches, can be a frustrating experience.

☞ What will they contribute to the business? For instance, a partner may bring in start-up money, facilities, or equipment. However, consider if this is enough of a reason to bring them on board. You may be able to get the same advantages in another way—for instance, renting a garage rather than working out of your partner's. Likewise, doubling skill sets does not always double productivity.

☞ Do they have any liabilities? For instance, if your prospective partner has declared bankruptcy in the past, this can hurt your collective venture's ability to get credit.

☞ Will the profits be able to sustain all the partners? Many start-up ventures do not turn profits immediately, and what little they do produce can be spread thin amongst many partners. Carefully work out the math.

Also bear in mind that going into business together can put a strain on even the best personal relationships. No matter whether it is family, friends, or strangers, keep everything very professional with written agreements regarding these investments. Get everything in writing, and be clear where obligations begin and end. "It's important to go into business with the right people," says Curtis. "If you don't—if it degrades into infighting and petty bickering—it can really go south quickly."

Incorporating. . . or Not

Think long and hard about incorporating. Starting a business often requires a fairly large—and risky—financial investment, which in turn exposes you to personal liability. Furthermore, as your business grows, so does your risk. Incorporating can help you shield yourself from this liability. However, it also has disadvantages.

To begin with, incorporating is not necessary for conducting professional transactions such as obtaining bank accounts and credit. You can do this as a sole proprietor, partnership, or simply by filing a DBA ("doing business as") statement with your local court (also known as "trading as" or an "assumed business name"). The DBA is an accounting entity that facilitates commerce and keeps your business' money separate from your own. However, the DBA does not shield you from responsibility if your business fails. It is entirely possible to ruin your credit, lose your house, and have your other assets seized in the unfortunate event of bankruptcy.

The purpose of incorporating is to shield yourself from personal financial liability. In case the worst happens, only the business' assets can be taken. However, this is not always the best solution. Check your local laws: Many states have laws that prevent a creditor from seizing a non-incorporated small business' assets in case of owner bankruptcy. If you are a corporation, however, the things you use to do business that are owned by the corporation—your office equipment, computers, restaurant refrigerators, and other essential equipment—may be seized by creditors, leaving you no way to work yourself out of debt. This is why it is imperative to consult with a lawyer.

There are other areas in which being a corporation can be an advantage, such as business insurance. Depending on your business needs, insurance can be for a variety of things: malpractice, against delivery failures or spoilage, or liability against defective products or accidents. Furthermore, it is easier to hire employees, obtain credit, and buy health insurance as an organization than as an individual. However, on the downside, corporations are subject to specific and strict laws concerning management and ownership. Again, you should consult with a knowledgeable legal expert.

Among the things you should discuss with your legal expert are the advantages and disadvantages of incorporating in your jurisdiction and which type of incorporation is best for you. The laws on liability and how much of your profit will be taken away in taxes vary widely by state and country. Generally, most small businesses owners opt for *limited liability companies* (LLCs), which gives them more control and a more flexible management structure. (Another possibility is a *limited liability partnership*, or *LLP*, which is especially useful for professionals such as doctors and lawyers.) Finally, there is the *corporation*, which is characterized by transferable ownerships shares, perpetual succession, and, of course, limited liability.

Most small businesses are sole proprietorships, partnerships, or privately-owned corporations. In the past, not many incorporated, since it was necessary to have multiple owners to start a corporation. However, this is changing, since it is now possible in many states for an individual to form a corporation. Note also that the form your business takes is usually not set in stone: A sole proprietorship or partnership can switch to become an LLC as it grows and the risks increase; furthermore, a successful LLC can raise capital by changing its structure to become a corporation and selling stock.

Legal Issues

Many other legal issues besides incorporating (or not) need to be addressed before you start your business. It is impossible to speak directly to every possible business need in this brief appendix, since regulations, licenses, and health and safety codes vary by industry and locality. A restaurant in Manhattan, for instance, has to deal not only with the usual issues such as health inspectors, the state liquor board, but obscure regulations such as New York City's cabaret laws, which prohibit dancing without a license in a place where alcohol is sold. An asbestos-abatement company, on the other hand, has a very different set of standards it has to abide by, including federal regulations. Researching applicable laws is part of starting up any business.

Part of being a wise business owner is knowing when you need help. There is software available for things like bookkeeping, business plans, and Web site creation, but generally, consulting with a knowledgeable professional—an accountant or a lawyer (or both)—is the smartest move. One of the most common mistakes is believing that just because you have expertise in the technical aspects of a certain field, you know all about running a business in that field. Whereas some people may balk at the expense, by suggesting the best way to deal with possible problems, as well as cutting through red tape and seeing possible pitfalls that you may not even have been aware of, such professionals usually more than make up for their cost. After all, they have far more experience at this than does a first-time business owner!

Financial

Another necessary first step in starting a business is obtaining a bank account. However, having the account is not as important as what you do with it. One of the most common problems with small businesses is undercapitalization—especially in brick-and-mortar businesses that sell or make something, rather than service-based businesses. The rule of thumb is that you should have access to money equal to your first year's anticipated profits, plus start-up expenses. (Note that this is not the same as having the money on hand—see the discussion on lines of credit, below.) For instance, if your annual rent, salaries, and equipment will cost $50,000 and you expect $25,000 worth of profit in your first year, you should have access to $75,000 worth of financing.

You need to decide what sort of financing you will need. Small business loans have both advantages and disadvantages. They can provide critical start-up credit, but in order to obtain one, your personal credit will need to be good, and you will, of course, have to pay them off with interest. In general, the more you and your partners put into the business yourselves, the more credit lenders will be willing to extend to you.

Equity can come from your own personal investment, either in cash or an equity loan on your home. You may also want to consider bringing on partners—at least limited financial partners—as a way to cover start-up costs.

It is also worth considering obtaining a line of credit instead of a loan. A loan is taken out all at once, but with a line of credit, you draw on the money as you need it. This both saves you interest payments and means that you have the money you need when you need it. Taking out too large of a loan can be worse than having no money at all! It just sits there collecting interest—or, worse, is spent on something utterly unnecessary—and then is not around when you need it most.

The first five years are the hardest for any business venture; your venture has about double the usual chance of closing in this time (1 out of 6, rather than 1 out of 12). You will probably have to tighten your belt at home, as well as work long hours and keep careful track of your business expenses. Be careful with your money. Do not take unnecessary risks, play it conservatively, and always keep some capital in reserve for emergencies. The hardest part of a new business, of course, is the learning curve of figuring out what, exactly, you need to do to make a profit, and so the best advice is to have plenty of savings—or a job to provide income—while you learn the ropes.

One thing you should not do is count on venture capitalists or "angel investors," that is, businesspeople who make a living investing on other businesses in the hopes that their equity in the company will increase in value. Venture capitalists have gotten something of a reputation as indiscriminate spendthrifts due to some poor choices made during the dot-com boom of the late 1990s, but the fact is that most do not take risks on unproven products. Rather, they are attracted to young companies that have the potential to become regional or national powerhouses and give better-than-average returns. Nor are venture capitalists are endless sources of money; rather, they are savvy businesspeople who are usually attracted to companies that have already experienced a measure of success. Therefore, it is better to rely on your own resources until you have proven your business will work.

Bookkeeping 101

The principles of double-entry bookkeeping have not changed much since its invention in the fifteenth century: one column records debits, and one records credits. The trick is *doing* it. As a small business owner, you need to be disciplined and meticulous at recording your finances. Thankfully, today there is software available that can do everything from tracking payables and receivables to running checks and generating reports.

Honestly ask yourself if you are the sort of person who does a good job keeping track of finances. If you are not, outsource to a bookkeeping company or hire someone to come in once or twice a week to enter invoices and generate checks for you. Also remember that if you have employees or even freelancers, you will have to file tax forms for them at the end of the year.

Another good idea is to have an accountant for your business to handle advice and taxes (federal, state, local, sales tax, etc.). In fact, consulting with an a certified public accountant is a good idea in general, since they are usually aware of laws and rules that you have never even heard of.

Finally, keep your personal and business accounting separate. If your business ever gets audited, the first thing the IRS looks for is personal expenses disguised as business expenses. A good accountant can help you to know what are legitimate business expenses. Everything you take from the business account, such as payroll and reimbursement, must be recorded and classified.

Being an Employer

Know your situation regarding employees. To begin with, if you have any employees, you will need an Employer Identification Number (EIN), also sometimes called a Federal Tax Identification Number. Getting an EIN is simple: You can fill out IRS form SS-4, or complete the process online at http://www.irs.gov.

Having employees carries other responsibilities and legalities with it. To begin with, you will need to pay payroll taxes (otherwise known as "withholding") to cover income tax, unemployment insurance, Social Security, and Medicare, as well as file W-2 and W-4 forms with the government. You will also be required to pay workman's compensation insurance, and will probably also want to find medical insurance. You are also required to abide by your state's nondiscrimination laws. Most states require you to post nondiscrimination and compensation notices in a public area.

Many employers are tempted to unofficially hire workers "off the books." This can have advantages, but can also mean entering a legal gray area. (Note, however, this is different from hiring freelancers, a temp employed by another company, or having a self-employed professional such as an accountant or bookkeeper come in occasionally to provide a service.) It is one thing to hire the neighbor's teenage son on a one-time basis to help you move some boxes, but quite another to have full-time workers working on a cash-and-carry basis. Regular wages must be noted in the accounts, and gaps may be questioned in the event of an audit. If the workers are injured on the job, you are not covered by workman's comp, and are thus vulnerable to lawsuits. If the workers you hired are not legal residents, you can also be liable for civil and criminal penalties. In general, it is best to keep your employees as above-board as possible.

Building a Business

Good business practices are essential to success. First off, do not overextend yourself. Be honest about what you can do and in what time frame. Secondly, be a responsible business owner. In general, if there is a problem, it is best to explain matters honestly to your clients than to leave them without word and wondering. In the former case, there is at least the possibility of salvaging your reputation and credibility.

Most business is still built by personal contacts and word of mouth. It is for this reason that maintaining your list of contacts is an essential practice. Even if a particular contact may not be useful at a particular moment, a future opportunity may present itself—or you may be able to send someone else to them. Networking, in other words, is as important when you are the boss as when you are looking for a job yourself. As the owner of a company, having a network means getting services on better terms, knowing where to go if you need help with a particular problem, or simply being in the right place at the right time to exploit an opportunity. Join professional organizations, the local Chamber of Commerce, clubs and community organizations, and learn to play golf. And remember—never burn a bridge.

Advertising is another way to build a business. Planning an ad campaign is not as difficult as you might think: You probably already know your media market and business community. The trick is applying it. Again, go with your instincts. If you never look twice at your local weekly, other people probably do not, either. If you are in a high-tourist area, though, local tourists maps might be a good way to leverage your marketing dollar. Ask other people in your area or market who have business similar to your own. Depending on your focus, you might want to consider everything from AM radio or local TV networks, to national trade publications, to hiring a PR firm for an all-out blitz. By thinking about these questions, you can spend your advertising dollars most effectively.

Nor should you underestimate the power of using the Internet to build your business. It is a very powerful tool for small businesses, potentially reaching vast numbers of people for relatively little outlay of money. Launching a Web site has become the modern equivalent of hanging out your shingle. Even if you are primarily a brick-and-mortar business, a Web presence can still be an invaluable tool—your store or offices will show up on Google searches, plus customers can find directions to visit you in person. Furthermore, the Internet offers the small-business owner many useful tools. Print and design services, order fulfillment, credit card processing, and networking—both personal and in terms of linking to other sites—are all available online. Web advertising can be useful, too, either by advertising on specialty sites that appeal to your audience, or by using services such as Google AdWords.

Amateurish print ads, TV commercials, and Web sites do not speak well of your business. Good media should be well-designed, well-edited, and well-put together. It need not, however, be expensive. Shop around and, again, use your network.

Flexibility is also important. "In general, a business must adapt to changing conditions, find new customers and find new products or services that customers need when the demand for their older products or services diminishes," says James Peck, a Long Island, New York, entrepreneur. In other words, if your original plan is not working out, or if demand falls, see if you can parlay your experience, skills, and physical plant into meeting other needs. People are not the only ones who can change their path in life; organizations can, too.

A Final Word

In business, as in other areas of life, the advice of more experienced people is essential. "I think it really takes three businesses until you know what you're doing," Drew Curtis confides. "I sure didn't know what I was doing the first time." Listen to what others have to say, no matter whether it is about your Web site or your business plan. One possible solution is seeking out a mentor, someone who has previously launched a successful venture in this field. In any case, before taking any step, ask as many people as many questions as you can. Good advice is invaluable.

Further Resources

American Independent Business Alliance
http://www.amiba.net

American Small Business League
http://www.asbl.com

IRS Small Business and Self-Employed One-Stop Resource
http://www.irs.gov/businesses/small/index.html

The Riley Guide: Steps in Starting Your Own Business
http://www.rileyguide.com/steps.html

Small Business Administration
http://www.sba.gov

Appendix B

Outfitting Yourself for Career Success

As you contemplate a career shift, the first component is to assess your interests. You need to figure out what makes you tick, since there is a far greater chance that you will enjoy and succeed in a career that taps into your passions, inclinations, natural abilities, and training. If you have a general idea of what your interests are, you at least know in which direction you want to travel. You may know you want to simply switch from one sort of nursing to another, or change your life entirely and pursue a dream you have always held. In this case, you can use a specific volume of The Field Guides to Finding a New Career to discover which position to target. If you are unsure of your direction you want to take, well, then the entire scope of the series is open to you! Browse through to see what appeals to you, and see if it matches with your experience and abilities.

The next step you should take is to make a list—do it once in writing—of the skills you have used in a position of responsibility that transfer to the field you are entering. People in charge of interviewing and hiring may well understand that the skills they are looking for in a new hire are used in other fields, but you must spell it out. Most job descriptions are partly a list of skills. Map your experience into that, and very early in your contacts with a prospective employer explicitly address how you acquired your relevant skills. Pick a relatively unimportant aspect of the job to be your ready answer for where you would look forward to learning within the organization, if this seems essentially correct. When you transfer into a field, softly acknowledge a weakness while relating your readiness to learn, but never lose sight of the value you offer both in your abilities and in the freshness of your perspective.

Energy and Experience

The second component in career-switching success is energy. When Jim Fulmer was 61, he found himself forced to close his piano-repair business. However, he was able to parlay his knowledge of music, pianos, and the musical instruments industry into another job as a sales representative for a large piano manufacturer, and quickly built up a clientele of musical-instrument retailers throughout the East Coast. Fulmer's experience highlights another essential lesson for career-changers: There are plenty of opportunities out there, but jobs will not come to you—especially the career-oriented, well-paying ones. You have to seek them out.

Jim Fulmer's case also illustrates another important point: Former training and experience can be a key to success. "Anyone who has to make a career change in any stage of life has to look at what skills they have acquired but may not be aware of," he says. After all, people can more easily change into careers similar to the ones they are leaving. Training and experience also let you enter with a greater level of seniority, provided you have the other necessary qualifications. For instance, a nurse who is already experienced with administering drugs and their benefits and drawbacks, and who is also graced with the personality and charisma to work with the public, can become a pharmaceutical company sales representative.

Unlock Your Network

The next step toward unlocking the perfect job is networking. The term may be overused, but the idea is as old as civilization. More than other animals, humans need one another. With the Internet and telephone, never in history has it been easier to form (or revive) these essential links. One does not have to gird oneself and attend reunion-type events (though for many this is a fine tactic)—but keep open to opportunities to meet people who may be friendly to you in your field. Ben Franklin understood the principal well—*Poor Richard's Almanac* is something of a treatise on the importance or cultivating what Franklin called "friendships" with benefactors. So follow in the steps of the founding fathers and make friends to get ahead. Remember: helping others feels good; it's often the receiving that gets a little tricky. If you know someone particularly well-connected in your field, consider tapping one or two less important connections first so that you make the most of the important one. As you proceed, keep your strengths foremost in your mind because the glue of commerce is mutual interest.

Eighty percent of job openings are *never advertised*, and, according to the U.S. Bureau of Labor statistics, more than half all employees landed their jobs through networking. Using your personal contacts is far more efficient and effective than trusting your résumé to the Web. On the Web, an employer needs to sort through tens of thousands—or millions—of résumés. When you direct your application to one potential employer, you are directing your inquiry to one person who already knows you. The personal touch is everything: Human beings are social animals, programmed to "read" body language; we are naturally inclined to trust those we meet in person, or who our friends and coworkers have recommended. While Web sites can be useful (for looking through help-wanted ads, for instance), expecting employers to pick you out of the slush pile is as effective as throwing your résumé into a black hole.

Do not send your résumé out just to make yourself feel like you're doing something. The proper way to go about things is to employ discipline and order, and then to apply your charm. Begin your networking efforts by making a list of people you can talk to: colleagues, coworkers, and supervisors, people you have had working relationship with, people from church, athletic teams, political organizations, or other community groups, friends, and relatives. You can expand your networking opportunities by following the suggestions in each chapter of the volumes. Your goal here is not so much to land a job as to expand your possibilities and knowledge: Though the people on your list may not be in the position to help you themselves, they might know someone who is. Meeting with them might also help you understand traits that matter and skills that are valued in the field in which you are interested. Even if the person is a potential employer, it is best to phrase your request as if you were seeking information: "You might not be able to help me, but do you know someone I could talk to who could tell me more about what it is like to work in this field?" Being hungry gives one impression, being desperate quite another.

Keep in mind that networking is a two-way street. If you meet someone who had an opening that is not right for you, but if you could recommend someone else, you have just added to your list two people who will be favorably disposed toward you in the future. Also, bear in mind that *you* can help people in *your* old field, thus adding to your own contacts list.

Networking is especially important to the self-employed or those who start their own businesses. Many people in this situation begin because they either recognize a potential market in a field that they are familiar with, or because full-time employment in this industry is no longer a possibility. Already being well-established in a field can help, but so can asking connections for potential work and generally making it known that you are ready, willing, and able to work. Working your professional connections, in many cases, is the *only* way to establish yourself. A free-lancer's network, in many cases, is like a spider's web. The spider casts out many strands, since he or she never knows which one might land the next meal.

Dial-Up Help

In general, it is better to call contacts directly than to e-mail them. E-mails are easy for busy people to ignore or overlook, even if they do not mean to. Explain your situation as briefly as possible (see the discussion of the "elevator speech"), and ask if you could meet briefly, either at their office or at a neutral place such as a café. (Be sure that you pay the bill in such a situation—it is a way of showing you appreciate their time and effort.) If you get someone's voicemail, give your "elevator speech" and then say you will call back in a few days to follow up—and then do so. If you reach your contact directly and they are too busy to speak or meet with you, make a definite appointment to call back at a later date. Be persistent, but not annoying.

Once you have arranged a meeting, prep yourself. Look at industry publications both in print and online, as well as news reports (here, GoogleNews, which lets you search through online news reports, can be very handy). Having up-to-date information on industry trends shows that you are dedicated, knowledgeable, and focused. Having specific questions on employers and requests for suggestions will set you apart from the rest of the job-hunting pack. Knowing the score—for instance, asking about the value of one sort of certification instead of another—pegs you as an "insider," rather than a dilettante, someone whose name is worth remembering and passing along to a potential employer.

Finally, set the right mood. Here, a little self-hypnosis goes a long way: Look at yourself in the mirror, and tell yourself that you are an enthusiastic, committed professional. Mood affects confidence and performance. Discipline your mind so you keep your perspective and self-respect. Nobody wants to hire someone who comes across as insincere, tells a sob story, or is still in the doldrums of having lost their previous job. At the end of any networking meeting, ask for someone else who might be able to help you in your journey to finding a position in this field, either with information or a potential job opening.

Get a Lift

When you meet with a contact in person (as well as when you run into anyone by chance who may be able to help you), you need an "elevator speech" (so-named because it should be short enough to be delivered during an elevator ride from a ground level to a high floor). This is a summary in which, in less than two minutes, you give them a clear impression of who you are, where you come from, your experience and goals, and why you are on the path you are on. The motto above Plato's Academy holds true: Know Thyself (this is where our Career Compasses and guides will help you). A long and rambling "elevator story" will get you nowhere. Furthermore, be positive: Neither a sad-sack story nor a tirade explaining how everything that went wrong in your old job is someone else's fault will get you anywhere. However, an honest explanation of a less-than-fortunate circumstance, such as a decline in business forcing an office closing, needing to change residence to a place where you are not qualified to work in order to further your spouse's career, or needing to work fewer hours in order to care for an ailing family member, is only honest.

An elevator speech should show 1) you know the business involved; 2) you know the company; 3) you are qualified (here, try to relate your education and work experience to the new situation); and 4) you are goal-oriented, dependable, and hardworking. Striking a balance is important; you want to sound eager, but not overeager. You also want to show a steady work experience, but not that you have been so narrowly focused that you cannot adjust. Most important is emphasizing what you can do for the company. You will be surprised how much information you can include in two minutes. Practice this speech in front of a mirror until you have the key points down perfectly. It should sound natural, and you should come across as friendly, confident, and assertive. Finally, remember eye contact! Good eye contact needs to be part of your presentation, as well as your everyday approach when meeting potential employers and leads.

Get Your Résumé Ready

Everyone knows what a résumé is, but how many of us have really thought about how to put one together? Perhaps no single part of the job search is subject to more anxiety—or myths and misunderstandings—than this 8 ½-by-11-inch sheet of paper.

On the one hand, it is perfectly all right for someone—especially in certain careers, such as academia—to have a résumé that is more than one page. On the other hand, you do not need to tell a future employer *everything*. Trim things down to the most relevant; for a 40-year-old to mention an internship from two decades ago is superfluous. Likewise, do not include irrelevant jobs, lest you seem like a professional career-changer.

Tailor your descriptions of your former employment to the particular position you are seeking. This is not to say you should lie, but do make your experience more appealing. If the job you're looking for involves supervising other people, say if you have done this in the past; if it involves specific knowledge or capabilities, mention that you possess these qualities. In general, try to make your past experience seem as similar to what you are seeking.

The standard advice is to put your Job Objective at the heading of the résumé. An alternative to this is a Professional Summary, which some recruiters and employers prefer. The difference is that a Job Objective mentions the position you are seeking, whereas a Professional Summary mentions your background (e.g. "Objective: To find a position as a sales representative in agribusiness machinery" versus "Experienced sales representative; strengths include background in agribusiness, as well as building team dynamics and market expansion"). Of course, it is easy to come up with two or three versions of the same document for different audiences.

The body of the résumé of an experienced worker varies a lot more than it does at the beginning of your career. You need not put your education or your job experience first; rather, your résumé should emphasize your strengths. If you have a master's degree in a related field, that might want to go before your unrelated job experience. Conversely, if too much education will harm you, you might want to bury that under the section on professional presentations you have given that show how good you are at communicating. If you are currently enrolled in a course or other professional development, be sure to note this (as well as your date of expected graduation). A résumé is a study of blurs, highlights, and jewels. You blur everything you must in order to fit the description of your experience to the job posting. You highlight what is relevant from each and any of your positions worth mentioning. The jewels are the little headers and such—craft them, since they are what is seen first.

You may also want to include professional organizations, work-related achievements, and special abilities, such as your fluency in a foreign language. Also mention your computer software qualifications and capabilities, especially if you are looking for work in a technological field or if you are an older job-seeker who might be perceived as behind the technology curve. Including your interests or family information might or might not be a good idea—no one really cares about your bridge club, and in fact they might worry that your marathon training might take away from your work commitments, but, on the other hand, mentioning your golf handicap or three children might be a good idea if your potential employer is an avid golfer or is a family woman herself.

You can either include your references or simply note, "References available upon request." However, be sure to ask your references' permission to use their names and alert them to the fact that they may be contacted before you include them on your résumé! Be sure to include name, organization, phone number, and e-mail address for each contact.

Today, word processors make it easy to format your résumé. However, beware of prepackaged résumé "wizards"—they do not make you stand out in the crowd. Feel free to strike out on your own, but remember the most important thing in formatting a résumé is consistency. Unless you have a background in typography, do not get too fancy. Finally, be sure to have someone (or several people!) read your résumé over for you.

For more information on résumé writing, check out Web sites such as http://www.resume.monster.com.

Craft Your Cover Letter

It is appropriate to include a cover letter with your résumé. A cover letter lets you convey extra information about yourself that does not fit or is not always appropriate in your résumé, such as why you are no longer working in your original field of employment. You can and should also mention the name of anyone who referred you to the job. You can go into some detail about the reason you are a great match, given the job description. Also address any questions that might be raised in the potential employer's mind (for instance, a gap in employment). Do not, however, ramble on. Your cover letter should stay focused on your goal: To offer a strong, positive impression of yourself and persuade the hiring manager that you are worth an interview. Your cover letter gives you a chance to stand out from the other applicants and sell yourself. In fact, according to a CareerBuilder.com survey, 23 percent of hiring managers say a candidate's ability to relate his or her experience to the job at hand is a top hiring consideration.

Even if you are not a great writer, you can still craft a positive yet concise cover letter in three paragraphs: An introduction containing the specifics of the job you are applying for; a summary of why you are a good fit for the position and what you can do for the company; and a closing with a request for an interview, contact information, and thanks. Remember to vary the structure and tone of your cover letter—do not begin every sentence with "I."

Ace Your Interview

In truth, your interview begins well before you arrive. Be sure to have read up well on the company and its industry. Use Web sites and magazines—http://www.hoovers.com offers free basic business information, and trade magazines deliver both information and a feel for the industries they cover. Also, do not neglect talking to people in your circle who might know about trends in the field. Leave enough time to digest the information so that you can give some independent thought to the company's history and prospects. You don't need to be an expert when you arrive to be interviewed; but you should be comfortable. The most important element of all is to be poised and relaxed during the interview itself. Preparation and practice can help a lot.

Be sure to develop well-thought-through answers to the following, typical interview openers and standard questsions.

☞ Tell me about yourself. (Do not complain about how unsatisfied you were in your former career, but give a brief summary of your applicable background and interest in the particular job area.) If there is a basis to it, emphasize how much you love to work and how you are a team player.

☞ Why do you want this job? (Speak from the brain, and the heart—of course you want the money, but say a little here about what you find interesting about the field and the company's role in it.)

☞ What makes you a good hire? (Remember here to connect the company's needs and your skill set. Ultimately, your selling points probably come down to one thing: you will make your employer money. You want the prospective hirer to see that your skills are valuable not to the world in general but to this specific company's bottom line. What can you do for them?)

☞ What led you to leave your last job? (If you were fired, still try say something positive, such as, "The business went through a challenging time, and some of the junior marketing people were let go.")

Practice answering these and other questions, and try to be genuinely positive about yourself, and patient with the process. Be secure but not cocky; don't be shy about forcing the focus now and then on positive contributions you have made in your working life—just be specific. As with the elevator speech, practice in front of the mirror.

A couple pleasantries are as natural a way as any to start the actual interview, but observe the interviewer closely for any cues to fall silent and formally begin. Answer directly; when in doubt, finish your phrase and look to the interviewer. Without taking command, you can always ask, "Is there more you would like to know?" Your attentiveness will convey respect. Let your personality show too—a positive attitude and a grounded sense of your abilities will go a long way to getting you considered. During the interview, keep your cell phone off and do not look at your watch. Toward the end of your meeting, you may be asked whether you have any questions. It is a good idea to have one or two in mind. A few examples follow:

☞ "What makes your company special in the field?"
☞ "What do you consider the hardest part of this position?"
☞ "Where are your greatest opportunities for growth?"
☞ "Do you know when you might need anything further from me?"

Leave discussion of terms for future conversations. Make a cordial, smooth exit.

Remember to Follow Up

Send a thank-you note. Employers surveyed by CareerBuilder.com in 2005 said it matters. About 15 percent said they would not hire someone who did not follow up with a thanks. And almost 33 percent would think less of a candidate. The form of the note does not much matter—if you know a manager's preference, use it. Otherwise, just be sure to follow up.

Winning an Offer

A job offer can feel like the culmination of a long and difficult struggle. So naturally, when you hear them, you may be tempted to jump at the offer. Don't. Once an employer wants you, he or she will usually give you a chance to consider the offer. This is the time to discuss terms of employment, such as vacation, overtime, and benefits. A little effort now can be well worth it in the future. Be sure to do a check of prevailing salaries for your field and area before signing on. Web sites for this include Payscale.com, Salary.com, and Salaryexpert.com. If you are thinking about asking for better or different terms from what the prospective employer offered, rest assured—that's how business gets done; and it may just burnish the positive impression you have already made.

Index

A

age group landmarks
    computer programmer, 10–11
    computer repair technician, 52
    computer software engineer, 42–43
    computer systems analyst, 30–32
    cyber security specialist, 62–63
    database administrator, 20–21
    forensic computing specialist, 95–96
    network administrator, 73
    systems engineer, 84–85
American Independent Business Alliance, 109
American Small Business League, 109
artificial intelligence, 2–3, 4
Association for Computing Machinery, 11
AWK, computer programming language, 9

B

Bachelor of Cybersecurity, 63
background/related work experience
    computer programmer, 6, 8–9
    computer repair technician, 51
    computer software engineer, 37
    computer systems analyst, 28
    cyber security specialist, 58–60
    forensic computing specialist, 91–92
    IT field and, xiv
    law enforcement, 58–59, 60, 63, 91
    military, 58, 60, 91, 92
    network administrator, 67, 68–69, 73
    systems engineer, 80, 82
Best Buy, 50
bookkeeping, 105–106
British Standards Institute, 56
Bureau of Labor Statistics, vii, viii
business, starting own, 99–109
    bookkeeping for, 105–106
    building, 107–108
    employer in, being, 106–107
    financial issues in, 104–105
    incorporation of, 102–103
    legal issues in, 103–104

    partnership in, 101–102
    plan, 99–101
    resources for, 109
    testimonial on, 113–114

C

C++, 3, 38
career(s)
    finding new, vii–vii, xi–xiii
    IT, xi–xiv, 13
    successful, 113–122
career compasses
    computer programmer, 2
    computer repair technician, 45
    computer software engineer, 34
    computer systems analyst, 23
    cyber security specialist, 55
    database administrator, 13
    forensic computing specialist, 87
    network administrator, 65
    systems engineer, 76
CareerBuilder.com, 122
CASE. *See* computer-assisted software
    engineering
CERT Coordination Center, 63
certification. *See* degrees/certification
civil service exam, 91, 95
COBOL, 3
College Board, 43
communication skills, xi, xii, 14, 16, 83
computer-assisted software engineering
    (CASE), 4–5
Computer Forensics 101, 96
computer programmer, 2–11
    age group landmarks for, 10–11
    background/related work experience, 6, 8–9
    career compasses for, 2
    degrees/certification of, 5, 6, 10
    education for, 6–7
    essential gear of, 3, 4
    field notes from, 8–9
    job description for, xi, 2–5

job market, 5
resources for, 5, 11
résumé for, 4
skills/qualifications of, 4, 6–7
transition expedition of, 7–10
computer programming languages, 3, 4, 5, 8, 9, 34, 36
ComputerRepair.com, 53
computer repair technician, 45–53
    age group landmarks for, 52
    background/related work experience of, 51
    career compasses for, 45
    degrees/certification of, 47–48, 51–52
    earnings of, 46, 50
    essential gear of, 46, 52
    field notes from, 51
    job description for, xiii–xiv, 45–48
    job market, 45–46, 47
    resources for, 50, 53
    retail employment and, 47
    skills/qualifications of, 48–49
    specialization, 48
    transition expedition of, 50–52
"Computer Repair Technician Jobs—Or Hire Yourself!", 53
computer software engineer, 34–43
    age group landmarks for, 42–43
    background/related work experience, 37
    career compasses for, 34
    degrees/certification of, 34, 42
    essential gear of, 35, 36
    field notes from, 40–41
    job description for, xiii, 34–38
    job market, 34, 38, 42
    resources for, 41, 43
    specialization, 39–40
    transition expedition of, 39–42
computer systems analyst, 23–32
    age group landmarks for, 30–32
    background/related work experience of, 28
    career compasses for, 23

degrees/certification of, 29–30
earnings of, 28
essential gear of, 24, 29
field notes from, 30–31
job description for, xiii, 23–26
job market, 24
job titles of, 25–26, 28–29
resources for, 32
résumé of, 24, 29, 32
skills/qualifications of, 26–27
specialization, 28
transition expedition of, 28–30
Control Engineering Virtual Library, 85
cover letter, 119–120
credit, financing and, 104–105
CSI, 87
cyber security, major aspects of, 56
Cyber Security Specialist, 63
cyber security specialist, xii, 55–63
    age group landmarks for, 62–63
    background/related work experience of, 58–60
    career compasses for, 55
    degrees/certification of, 58, 59, 62
    essential gear of, 56, 62
    field notes from, 61
    job description for, 55–58
    job market, 60
    job titles for, 60
    privacy concerns for, 62
    public service and, 62
    relocation issues for, 61
    resources for, 63
    skills/qualifications of, 57–58, 59
    transition expedition of, 60–62

D

database administrator (DBA), xi–xii, 13–21
    age group landmarks for, 20–21
    career compasses for, 13
    degrees/certification of, 16, 19–20
    earnings of, 15–16

essential gear of, 14, 20
field notes from, 18–19
job description for, xi, 13–17
job market, 13
resources for, 21
résumé of, 20, 21
skills/qualifications of, 14
specialization and, 17, 18
transition expedition of, 17–20
database software
filemaker, 21
Oracle, 3, 17, 18, 20, 21
data recovery, 48
A Day in the Life-Computer Software Engineer, 43
DBA. *See* database administrator
degrees/certification. *See also* skills/ qualifications
computer programmer, 5, 6, 10
computer repair technician, 47–48, 51–52
computer software engineer, 34, 42
computer systems analyst, 29–30
cyber security specialist, 58, 59, 62
database administrator, 16, 19–20
forensic computing specialist, 94–95
Microsoft, 21, 85
network administrator, 67, 68, 72–73
systems engineer, 78, 80, 82, 84
Dice, 43
diversity concerns, 38
Dream.In.Code, 5

E

earnings
computer repair technician, 46, 50
computer systems analyst, 28
database administrator, 15–16
IT career, xiv
job offers and, 122
network administrator, 67
EDD. *See* Electronic Data Discovery

education, 21. *See also* degrees/certification
computer programmer, 6–7
scams in forensic computing specialist, 94–95
systems engineer, 78, 81–82
Education Portal, 63
Electronic Data Discovery (EDD), 94–95
elevator speech, 117
employer, starting own business as, 106–107
energy, 113–114
engineering. *See also* computer software engineer; systems engineer
fields in, 83
equity, business and, 104
essential gear
computer programmer, 3, 4
computer repair technician, 46, 52
computer software engineer, 35, 36
computer systems analyst, 24, 29
cyber security specialist, 56, 62
database administrator, 14, 20
forensic computing specialist, 88, 90
network administrator, 66, 72
systems engineer, 77, 78
experience, career success and, 113–114

F

FACT. *See* Forensic Association of Computer Technologists
field notes
business, starting own, 113–114
computer programmer, 8–9
computer repair technician, 51
computer software engineer, 40–41
computer systems analyst, 30–31
cyber security specialist, 61
database administrator, 18–19
forensic computing specialist, 94–95
network administrator, 70–71
systems engineer, 82–83
fifties, age group

computer programmers in, 11
computer repair technicians in, 52
computer software engineers in, 43
computer systems analysts in, 31
cyber security specialists in, 63
database administrators in, 21
forensic computing specialists in, 96
network administrators in, 73
systems engineers in, 85
Filemaker, 21
financial considerations, business and, 104–105
follow up, interview, 122
Forensic Association of Computer Technologists (FACT), 96
forensic computing specialist, 87–96
    age group landmarks for, 95–96
    background/related work experience of, 91–92
    career compasses for, 87
    degrees/certification of, 94–95
    education scams for, 94–95
    essential gear of, 88, 90
    field notes from, 94–95
    job description for, xii, 87–91
    job titles for, 93
    law enforcement and, 88, 91, 92, 93, 94, 95–96
    privacy concerns for, 88
    resources for, 96
    skills/qualifications of, 91–92
    television glorification of, xii, 90
    transition expedition of, 92–95
forensics, 88–89, 90
FORTRAN, 9, 36
Franklin, Benjamin, *Poor Richard's Almanac*, 114

G

Geek Squad, 50, 53
Google, computer programmer for, 8–9
Guide to Career Education, 21

H

hacking, 59
HTCIA. *See* International High Technology Crime Investigation Association

I

IDEF. *See* Integration Definition
IEEE Computer Society, 11
incorporation, 102–103
INCOSE. *See* International Council on Systems Engineering
Indeed.com, 53
Information Systems Security Association (ISSA), 63
information technology (IT)
    careers in, xi–xiv, 13
    military use of, xii, 47, 57, 78, 83, 93
    volunteer positions in, 60, 71
Integration Definition (IDEF), 78
International Council on Systems Engineering (INCOSE), 84, 85
International High Technology Crime Investigation Association (HTCIA), 96
International Information Systems Security Certification Consortium (ISC), 58
interview, 120–122
IRS Small Business and Self-employed One-Stop Resource, 109
ISC. *See* International Information Systems Security Certification Consortium
IT. *See* information technology

J

Java, 3, 8, 34, 38
job(s)
    changing, vii–viii
    loss of, statistics on, vii
    offer, 122
job descriptions
    computer programmer, xi, 2–5
    computer repair technician, xiii–xiv, 45–48
    computer software engineer, xiii, 34–38

computer systems analyst, xiii, 23–26
cyber security specialist, xii, 55–58
database administrator, xi, 13–17
forensic computing specialist, xii, 87–91
network administrator, xii, 65–68
systems engineer, xiii, 76–80
job market
computer programmer, 5
computer repair technician, 45–46, 47
computer software engineer, 34, 38, 42
computer systems analyst, 24
cyber security specialist, 60
database administrator, 13
network administrator, 67–68
job titles
computer systems analyst, 25–26, 28–29
cyber security specialist, 60
forensic computing specialist, 93
network administrator, 65–66
Jobs for Programmers, 11

L

languages
AWK, 9
computer programming, 3, 4, 5, 8, 9, 34, 36
systems engineering, 78
law enforcement, xii, 58–59, 60, 63, 88, 91
forensics computing specialist and, 88, 91,
92, 93, 94, 95–96
leadership, 77, 83
The League of Professional System
Administrators, 74
legal issues, business, 103–104
Lehmer, Derrick Henry, 8

M

Mac, 57–58
MacPaint, 40, 41
malware, 57
mathematical skills, viii, xi, 6, 8, 27
MCSE. *See* Microsoft Certified Systems Engineer
microbusinesses, 99
Microsoft, certification by, 21, 85

Microsoft Certified Systems Engineer (MCSE), 85
Microsoft SQL Server Certification, 21
military
background/work experience in, 58, 60, 91,
92
IT and, xii, 47, 57, 78, 83, 93

N

National Workforce Center for Emerging
Technologies, 11
NetAdminTools.com, 74
network administrator, 65–74
age group landmarks for, 73
background/related work experience, 67,
68–69, 73
career compasses for, 65
degrees/certification of, 67, 68, 72–73
earnings of, 67
essential gear of, 66, 72
field notes from, 70–71
job description for, xii, 65–68
job market, 67–68
job titles for, 65–66
resources for, 71, 74
résumé of, 70, 71, 73
skills/qualifications of, 72
transition expedition of, 69–73
Network Administrator Skills Assessment Test,
74
The Network Administrator.com, 74
networking, 114–116
New Technologies, Inc. (NTI), 96
Novell, 73
NTI. *See* New Technologies, Inc.

O

O*NET Code Connector, 32
Oracle, 3, 17, 18, 20, 21

P

partners, business, 101–102
Poor Richard's Almanac (Franklin), 114
privacy, xii, 62, 88
public service, cyber security specialist and, 62

Q

QFD. *See* Quality Function Deployment
Quality Function Deployment (QFD), 78

R

relocation issues, cyber security specialist, 61
repetitive stress injuries, 17
resources
    business, starting own, 109
    computer programmer, 5, 11
    computer repair technician, 50, 53
    computer software engineer, 41, 43
    computer systems analyst, 32
    cyber security specialist, 63
    database administrator, 21
    forensic computing specialist, 96
    IT volunteering, 60, 71, 73
    Job offer/salary-related, 122
    network administrator, 71, 74
    systems engineer, 83, 84, 85
résumé, 118–119
    computer programmer, 4
    computer systems analyst, 24, 29, 32
    cover letter for, 119–120
    database administrator, 20, 21
    network administrator, 70, 71, 73
    systems engineer, 84
retail, computer repair technician, 47
The Riley Guide: Steps in Starting Your Own
    Business, 109

S

salary. *See* earnings
SC Magazine, 63
scams, education, 94–95
security standards, 56
self promotion, computer programmer, 4
sixties plus, age group
    computer programmers in, 11
    computer repair technicians in, 52
    computer software engineers in, 43
    computer systems analysts in, 31–32

cyber security specialists in, 63
database administrators in, 21
forensic computing specialists in, 96
network administrators in, 73
systems engineers in, 85
skills/qualifications
    communication, xi, xii, 14, 16, 83
    computer programmer, 4, 6–7
    computer repair technician, 48–49
    computer systems analyst, 26–27
    cyber security specialist, 57–58, 59
    database administrator, 14
    forensic computing specialist, 91–92
    IT, xi, xiii
    leadership, 77, 83
    mathematical, viii, xi, 6, 8, 27
    network administrator, 72
    systems engineer, 77, 80–81
Small Business Administration, 109
Software Engineering Institute, 32
software quality assurance analyst, 25–26
software testing, 37
specialization
    computer repair technician, 48
    computer software engineer, 39–40
    computer systems analyst, 28
    database administrator, 17, 18
SQL, 18
standards, security, 56
statistics, job loss, vii
success, outfitting for career, 113–122
    energy/experience for, 113–114
Sybase, 3, 18
system architect, 25
Systems Analysis Web sites, 32
systems engineer, 76–85
    age group landmarks for, 84–85
    background/related work experience of, 80, 82
    career compasses for, 76
    degrees/certification of, 78, 80, 82, 84

education of, 78, 81–82
engineering fields related to, 83
essential gear of, 77, 78
field notes from, 82–83
job description for, xiii, 76–80
resources for, 83, 84, 85
résumé of, 84
skills/qualifications of, 77
tools/languages developed for, 78
transition expedition of, 81–84
SystemsEngineerJobs.com, 83

T

technical process models, 79
TechRepublic, 74
telephone skills, 116–117
television, forensics glorified by, xii, 90
testing. *See* software testing
thirties/forties, age group
computer programmers in, 10–11
computer repair technicians in, 52
computer software engineers in, 43
computer systems analysts in, 31
cyber security specialists in, 62–63
database administrators in, 21
forensic computing specialists in, 95–96
network administrators in, 73
systems engineers in, 84
transition expedition
computer programmer, 7–10
computer repair technician, 50–52
computer software engineer, 39–42
computer systems analyst, 28–30

cyber security specialist, 60–62
database administrator, 17–20
forensic computing specialist, 92–95
network administrator, 69–73
systems engineer, 81–84
trojan horses, 56–57
twenties, age group
computer programmers in, 10
computer repair technicians in, 52
computer software engineers in, 42
computer systems analysts in, 30–31
cyber security specialists in, 62
database administrators in, 20
forensic computing specialists in, 95
network administrators in, 73
systems engineers in, 84

U

UML. *See* Unified Modeling Language
Unified Modeling Language (UML), 78

V

Virtual Skies Career Radar: Computer Software
    Engineer, 43
viruses, 57
V-Model, 79
volunteering, 60, 71, 73

W

waterfall model, 79
"What is Systems Engineering?: A Consensus of
    Senior Systems Engineers," 85
Worldwide Institute of Software Architecture,
    32
worms, 57